W9-AOM-259

MENUS THAT MADE HISTORY

FOR HILARY, HOLLY AND ISAAC
AND
FOR PHILIP AND PHYLLIS,
WILMA, ROBERT, EDWARD, AND THOMAS

An Hachette UK Company
www.hachette.co.uk

First published in Great Britain in 2019 by
Kyle Books, an imprint of Kyle Cathie Ltd
Carmelite House
50 Victoria Embankment
London EC4Y 0DZ
www.kylebooks.co.uk

ISBN: 978 0 85783 528 4

Back cover images (left to right): Archive PL/Alamy Stock Photo; Interfoto/Alamy Stock Photo; Academia Barilla Gastronomic Library, Parma

Distributed in the US by Hachette Book Group, 1290 Avenue of the Americas, 4th and 5th Floors, New York, NY 10104

Distributed in Canada by Canadian Manda Group, 664 Annette St., Toronto, Ontario, Canada M6S 2C8

Publisher: Joanna Copestick
Editor: Hannah Coughlin
Design: Rachel Cross
Recipe development: Sophie Wright
Production: Allison Gonsalves

A Cataloguing in Publication record for this title is available from the British Library

Printed and bound in Italy

MENUS THAT MADE HISTORY

Over 2000 years of menus from Ancient Egyptian food for the afterlife to Elvis Presley's wedding breakfast

VINCENT FRANKLIN
& ALEX JOHNSON

KYLE BOOKS

Vegetarierheim"
Vegetarisches Speisehaus Abstinenz-C
Speise-Karte.
Zürich, den 6. November 1898.
Suppe:
Kraftbrühe m. Einlage 15
Körner- und Hülsenfrüchte:
Weisse Bohnen 15
Salate
Kopfsalat (mit Ei 35) 20
Karottensalat 20
Rettichsalat 20
Gemischten-Salat 20
Rosenkohl
Gemüse:
Kohlrabi
Mehlspeisen:
Gries in Milch mit Obst
Strudel gefüllt
Gugelhopf
Äpfel im Schlafrock
Obst und Kompots:
Zwetschgen
Äpfel
SOUVENIR
First Battalion A.I.F.
Association
Re-Union - - Smoko
20 - 10 - 28
COCOA TREE CAFE
WELCOME
SUPPER
Beer
Sandwiches
Beer
Hot Sausage Rolls
Beer
Biscuits and Cheese
LLA RUSSA di 50. COPERTI dato dal CORPO DECURIONALE
DELLA CITTÀ DI TORINO
SERVITO DA BER.do TROMBETTA.
per Mercoledì 1.º Marzo 1848.
Zuppa di Testuggine
ANTIPASTO.
Fritto misto.
Pesce Turbot a due salse.
Arrosto di Bue all' Inglese (quello del 1.º premio)
Cappone con tartuffi alla Parigina
Certosa di selvaggina
PUNCH ALLA ROMANA.
Piccoli piselli all' Inglese.
Carciofi alla Lionese.
Faggiano allo spiedo con crescione.
Pasticcio di feggato grasso con gelatina.
Plum-pudding al Rhum.
Crema alla Chantilly.
GELATI.
VIVA CARLO
VIVA L'ITALIA
Vegetarisch
Hiltl
VEGETARIERHEIM · CONDITOREI-CAFÉ

CONTENTS

INTRODUCTION 6

TRAVEL AND ADVENTURE 8

CAFÉS AND RESTAURANTS 34

ROYAL AND POLITICAL 60

FEAST AND CELEBRATIONS 88

SPORTS AND ENTERTAINMENT 104

WAR AND PEACE 122

ANCIENT AND CLASSICAL 144

ART AND LITERATURE 160

FAITH AND BELIEF 178

PRISONS AND INSTITUTIONS 192

WEIRD AND WONDERFUL 204

INDEX 222

ACKNOWLEDGEMENTS 224

INTRODUCTION

Menus are much more than mere lists of dishes. From the dawn of mankind to the present day, these everyday and often overlooked items have extraordinary stories to tell. They open doors to scenes of extravagance and austerity, migration and assimilation, war and conquest.

The word menu itself comes from a French term indicating something 'small' or 'detailed', and further back from the Latin *minutus*, used to describe an item that has been reduced in size. Four thousand years ago, in ancient Mesopotamia, people were putting together divine menus on clay tablets for their gods (who apparently enjoyed roast goat, cakes and plenty of salt, washed down with substantial amounts of alcohol). In China, menus for high days and holidays are found during the Song Dynasty (960–1279), including various impressive selections in one semi-anonymous civil servant's twelfth-century memoir, *Dreams of Splendour of the Eastern Capital*. The earliest European menus appeared in France in the eighteenth century: huge broadsheet-sized pieces of paper, crammed with hundreds of dishes in tiny print that made them look like a prototype classified ads section.

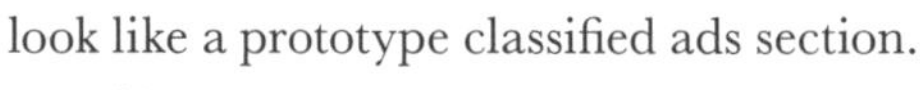

Since then, we have seen the arrival of highly decorated menu cards, menus that come in their own leather binding with tassels, handwritten menus, children's menus, even edible menus. And as with other ephemera such as football cards, postcards or film posters, people are starting to realise that menus offer us the chance to understand the past in ways we've never previously considered.

We eat to survive and we eat to celebrate. But this is not really a book about food – it's about

understanding what these culinary snapshots can tell us about certain times and places in our global history.

With over 40,000 years to pick from, it's been tricky weighing up which selections to serve and which to send back, whittling it down to the most fascinating. Yes, there has to be a place for ridiculously over-the-top royal banquets. But we've spread the net far wider than that. From Aztec cannibals to Swiss vegetarians, and from the first meal in space to the last one on the *Titanic*, the following pages even feature menus that were never actually cooked and served – the Cratchits of Dickens' *A Christmas Carol* only ever celebrated 25 December on the page.

Before the middle of the nineteenth century, very few of these menus were written down. So while the more modern ones may have been propped up against the salt and pepper pots, others have been pieced together from instructions to kitchens, accounts in diaries and even scientific research into the dental plaque of ancient corpses.

Together, they form an à la carte selection that reveals something unexpected, curious or just plain shocking about the people who prepared them, the people who ate them and the worlds they lived in. After you've read this book, you'll never look at a pineapple in the same way again.

CHAPTER ONE

TRAVEL AND ADVENTURE

FROM RECORD-BREAKING CANAPÉS IN THE AIR TO AN IRONIC ICE TWIST ABOARD THE TITANIC, THIS CHAPTER ALSO SHOWS YOU HOW TO COOK A WALRUS, REVEALS THE FATAL RESULTS OF GETTING A MENU VERY WRONG INDEED, AND EXPLAINS WHY CHILLI SAUCE IS SO POPULAR IN SPACE.

DINNER ON THE ORIENT EXPRESS

Paris to Constantinople, 17 April, 1884

In 1883, engineer and entrepreneur Georges Nagelmackers started running a luxury train service aimed at wealthy travellers looking for considerable comfort as they made their way across Europe. The Orient Express quickly became a byword for lavishness, using the white heat of late nineteenth-century technology to provide passengers with central heating, gas lighting and hot water on board. Essentially, it was a five-star hotel on wheels.

The opulence stretched to the restaurant car, where renowned French glass designer René Lalique was brought in to decorate the walls with glass panels inlaid in Cuban mahogany. The ceiling was covered with embossed leather from Cordoba, the walls with tapestries, and the tables in white damask with intricately folded napkins, crystal goblets and silver cutlery. In a series of first-hand reports from the inaugural journey, the Paris correspondent of *The Times*, journalist Henri Opper de Blowitz – who compared it to a banqueting hall – noted that the curtains of the restaurant car were deliberately raised before the train's departure so that onlookers could see what they were missing out on.

MENU

Potage

Perles du Japon

Poissons

Pommes à l'anglaise

Filet de bœuf Jardinière

Roti

Poulet du Mans au cresson

Legumes

Chou-fleur au gratin

Crème chocolat

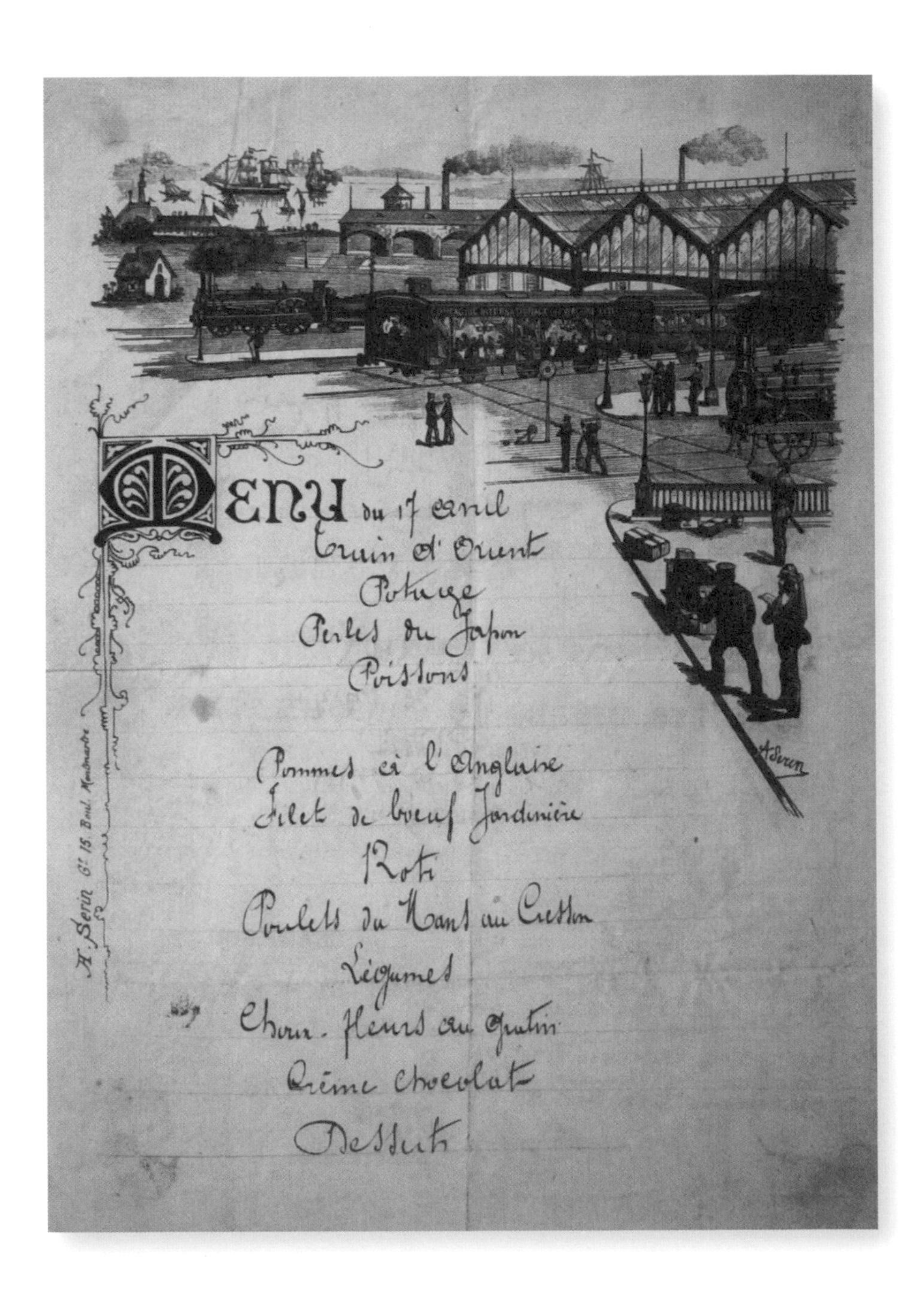

MENU du 17 Avril
Train d'Orient
Potage
Perles du Japon
Poissons

Pommes à l'Anglaise
Filet de boeuf Jardinière
Roti
Poulets du Mans au Cresson
Légumes
Choux-fleurs au Gratin
Crême chocolat
Desserts

A. Serin Gr. 15. Boul. Montmartre

A. Serin

Blowitz was also impressed with the menus, prepared en route in the tiny kitchen at the end of the dining car, which he said 'vie with each other in variety and sophistication'. However, the impressive-sounding French terminology masks what to 21st-century ears sounds a little on the nursery food side – *perles du Japon* is tapioca, *pommes à l'anglais* are boiled potatoes and *chou-fleur au gratin* is cauliflower cheese.

But the menu also featured one of the most popular dinner centrepieces of the age, *filet de bœuf jardinière*. It was a classic of French haute cuisine and made it onto the menu of the extravagant Bradley-Martin Ball at the Waldorf in New York in 1897. The larded, roasted and glazed filet was presented on a long dish, often raised on a special pastry frame or a bed of rice for added grandeur, then surrounded with vegetables (the 'jardinière' element including cauliflower, carrots, and beans) arranged in alternating colours. The whole thing was held together with special 'hatelet' or 'attelet' skewers which had highly decorative tops. It was served with a béarnaise sauce.

Menus in the 20th century continued to impress. In 1907, passengers would start their meal with scrambled eggs with truffles, moving on to foie gras aspic, and roasted Styrian goose. By 1925, they could also enjoy a classic French dish, *glace plombières*. This ice cream-based desert was laden with candied fruits (think 'tutti frutti' flavour) and built within a huge metal mould. There was also an attempt to reflect the train's geographic location with the food, so for example local tokay wine was served while crossing Hungary. One story has it that when a chef ran out of a certain ingredient on board, he would write down his request on a slip of paper, stick it in a hollow potato and when they pulled in to a station lob it at a member of the railway staff, who would ensure it would then be on hand at the following stop.

The Orient Express went through various regenerations throughout the years – by the time American travel writer Paul Theroux stepped aboard in 1975 he sadly discovered there was no restaurant car at all – and made its final overnight run in 2009. In its place today is the privately-run Venice Simplon-Orient-Express which includes vintage restored restaurant cars. Its current menu still

Tourist poster for the Orient Express, 1898.

includes chicken, but without the popular watercress option of 1884. Nowadays it is braised with morel sauce. And if you have a spare €490, you can also enjoy 50g of Petrossian Beluga caviar. ◈

FILLET OF BEEF WITH BALSAMIC ROASTED POTATOES, SHALLOTS AND GARLIC SAUCE

SERVES 6

For the beef fillet
800g (28oz) middle cut beef fillet
flaked sea salt and pepper
2 tablespoons vegetable oil
2 sprigs rosemary
1½ tablespoons butter

For the potatoes and shallots
800g (28oz) Maris Piper potatoes, skin on, cut into 6–8 wedges
6 banana shallots, peeled and cut in half (or 4 red onions, peeled and cut into wedges)
1 whole garlic bulb, cut across the equator
2 sprigs rosemary, finely chopped
100ml (3½ fl oz) balsamic vinegar
2 tablespoons unsalted butter
40g (1½oz) rocket

For the garlic sauce
150g (5oz) crème fraîche
juice 1 lemon
1 tablespoon Dijon mustard
salt and pepper

Preheat the oven to 190°C/170°C fan/370°F/gas mark 4.

Place the potato wedges onto a non-stick baking sheet along with the halved shallots or quartered red onions. Add the halved garlic bulbs, chopped rosemary and season generously with salt and pepper. Add the balsamic vinegar and dot with butter. Place the tray into the preheated oven and set the timer for 40 minutes.

Prepare the beef by seasoning it well on all sides with flaked sea salt and lots of black pepper.

Place a large skillet or frying pan onto your stove and turn the heat to high. Add the vegetable oil and when hot, lay in the beef fillet and add the rosemary sprigs. Cook for 6–7 minutes per side until it starts to become well browned and caramelised. Do this on all sides including the ends. Add the butter and baste the beef for a further 5 minutes. When well browned, remove the beef from the pan.

Remove the potatoes from the oven after 30–35 minutes. If there are some bits that are burning, move them around and the under-done bits to the side of the tray. Make some space in the centre for the beef fillet. Put the tray back into the oven and cook for a further 15 minutes for medium rare, 20 minutes for medium and 25–30 minutes for well done.

Bring the tray back out of the oven and allow the beef to rest while you make the sauce.

Remove the garlic heads from the tray which should now be soft and caramelised. Squeeze the garlic into a small bowl and mash with the back of a fork. Spoon in the crème fraîche, lemon juice, dijon mustard and the salt and pepper and stir well.

When the beef has had 10–15 minutes resting, arrange the potatoes and shallots onto a large platter and top with the rocket. Slice the beef and serve on warm plates with a spoonful of the garlic sauce.

DINNER TO HONOUR ROBERT PEARY (PROBABLY) REACHING THE NORTH POLE

1909

SIX MONTHS AFTER EXPLORER ROBERT EDWIN PEARY CLAIMED TO HAVE become the first person to reach the North Pole, *The New York Times* organised an Arctic-themed dinner to celebrate the achievement. While some courses were quite conventional – local oysters, petit fours and roast partridge – diners were treated to main courses well outside their comfort zone.

The standard daily ration on the final push for the Pole was 2lb 4½oz (just over 1kg) of solids per man, per day. Pemmican (see page 16) was the main food source, followed in order of importance by tea, condensed milk, biscuit and compressed pea soup. So pemmican was an obvious inclusion for the congratulatory dinner, though in a more palatable mousse form and served in Hungarian 'Kossuth' style with spinach and paprika.

On his expedition, Peary had taken two types of pemmican, a fruit-cake version and the traditional beef-fat mixture. He loved it: 'Of all the foods that I am acquainted with,' he wrote, 'pemmican is the only one that, under appropriate conditions, a man can eat twice a day for three hundred and sixty-five days in a year and have the last mouthful taste as good as the first.' However, when he appeared before the Naval Affairs Subcommittee of the US House of Representatives two years later to gain official accreditation for the expedition, Representative Henry T. Helgesen of North Dakota wondered why his diary lacked the greasy hand marks pemmican left behind. Helgesen's pemmican-related doubts, which went so far as to backing an alternative candidate as the 'first to the pole', counted for nothing and Peary's claim was eventually approved.

Also a bit greasy is walrus, even when enjoyed, as it was at the dinner, in thin slices. A traditional Alaskan subsistence food, it must be cooked thoroughly, otherwise you risk becoming infected with a worm called trichinella which can leave you very ill indeed (although igunaq – raw, fermented walrus meat stored

Arctic-themed dinner to celebrate Robert Peary.

underground for months – is an Inuit delicacy, it was not served). Similarly slippery is narwhal, served with the blubber or *mattak* attached.

Some diners may have preferred the little less challenging Inuit favourite of musk-ox fillets (looks like beef, tastes like horse), prepared Victoria-style with a sauce of black truffles, perhaps some lobster, and potato balls in clarified butter.

Peary's African-American right-hand man, Matthew Henson, was also arguably the first person to reach the North Pole, but his contribution was largely ignored and there was certainly no *New York Times* dinner to celebrate his efforts.

MENU

Blue Point oysters

Petite bouchée walrus

Velouté ptarmigan aux croutons

Suprême de narwhal Véronique

Mignon de musk ox Victoria

Pommes parisiennes

Mousse de pemmican Kossuth

Epinards aux fleurons

Sorbet 'North Pole'

Perdreau roti, bardé aux feuilles de vigne

Coeur de romaine en salade

Biscuit glacé Knickerbocker

Corbeille de mignardises

CAPTAIN SCOTT'S CHRISTMAS DINNER

1911

Celebrating midwinter in their wooden hut at Cape Evans in June 1911, Captain Robert Falcon Scott and his fellow explorers enjoyed a Christmas meal in the depths of the Antarctic cold. Starting with seal soup, they moved on to roast beef and Yorkshire pudding with fried potatoes and brussels sprouts, followed by flaming plum pudding, mince pies, anchovies, burnt almonds, crystallised fruits and chocolates, all washed down with champagne. Henry 'Birdie' Bowers even made a Christmas tree out of twigs and decorated it with candles and coloured paper. There were 'a few bad heads in the morning', Scott wrote in his diary.

Six months later, on 25 December, the celebrations were not so extravagant. At this point in their bid to reach the South Pole, the team's dogs had been sent back and the last ponies had been shot. It was now just the men on foot. Despite high winds and snowfall, they managed to walk 25km on Christmas Day before stopping for dinner in their tents. Earlier they had each enjoyed an extra piece of chocolate and two raisins in their tea as a special Yuletide treat. Outside it was around −25°C.

The main dish was pemmican, a concentrate of fat and ground, dried horsemeat which was invented by Native Americans and later adopted by fur traders and polar explorers as a high-energy food. Taste depends on the ingredients, but it has been compared to biting into a candle. This was supplemented by the 'hoosh', essentially a thick stew, and the psychologically rewarding dessert (several years earlier in his bid for the South Pole, Ernest Shackleton had hidden a Christmas pudding and a piece of holly in his socks). This amounted to about 16sq cm of plum pudding, according to the diary of one of the men, William Lashly, who had very nearly fallen into a crevasse earlier in the day. And finally four small pieces of caramel and four squares of ginger. 'I positively could not eat all mine,' wrote Lashly, 'and turned in feeling as if I had made a beast of myself.' Scott felt the same. 'After the feast it was difficult to move,' he wrote. 'We have all slept splendidly and feel thoroughly warm – such is the effect of full feeding.'

Scott's team got their menus seriously wrong, however. While there were three-course meals of turtle soup and penguin breast back at Cape Evans, the organisers had significantly underestimated what was needed for the final push. Their deliberately high-protein diet should have been high-fat for added energy, and they were taking in only about half the calories they needed to maintain their weight. Their vitamin B levels were also insufficient. Rations ran out quicker than expected and their dreams were filled with the promise of delicious titbits. They were literally starving. Meanwhile, while Scott's men ate white bread and pemmican, on the rival Amundsen expedition there was special brown bread, seal and berry preserves. No festive treats were included in Amundsen's rations.

As Christmas Day came to an end, Scott and his men were still nearly 500km from the pole. Amundsen had already reached it and was on his way back.

MENU

Pemmican, with slices of horse meat flavoured with onion and curry powder and thickened with biscuit

Arrowroot, cocoa and biscuit hoosh, sweetened

Plum pudding

Cocoa with raisins

Caramels and crystallised ginger

Robert Forde, Frank Debenham, Tryggve Gran and Griffith Taylor of The Second Western Party

RMS *TITANIC*'S LAST MENUS

14 April 1912

On 10 April 1912, RMS *Titanic* left Southampton, bound for Belfast and New York. Four days into her voyage, on the eve of disaster, she was serving up the kind of opulence for which the Edwardians are renowned. At least, she was serving it up in first class.

The distinction between the three classes of passenger is evident not only in the content of the menus – gruel in third, foie gras in first – but in the design too. First and second-class menus were printed in colour, with a different menu for each meal. Third-class had one, printed in black and white, for the whole day.

The social distinctions can also be seen in the words used to describe the different meals of the day. In third-class, 'dinner' was served in the middle of the day when other passengers were enjoying 'luncheon'. And while third-class passengers were having their 'tea', first class were sitting down to an 11-course 'dinner'. These words still define class distinctions and stir up social prejudices today. For some, 'supper' is a bit of a cheese and a cracker, or maybe a Weetabix. For others, it's an informal social event that often takes place close to an Aga.

Third-class is also the only menu that gives instructions on how to complain about the food, the service or 'incivility'. Why White Star felt these instructions necessary isn't clear. Perhaps they assumed first- and second-class passengers would be familiar with dining out and what to do if they were unhappy. Maybe they thought the level of service provided in third class was more likely to cause complaints. Or perhaps they were concerned that dissatisfied diners on the lower decks might resort to a more physical method of expressing themselves than others.

The food served on board a ship has always depended hugely on the technology available for preservation and storage. Even in 1912, the *Titanic's* menu

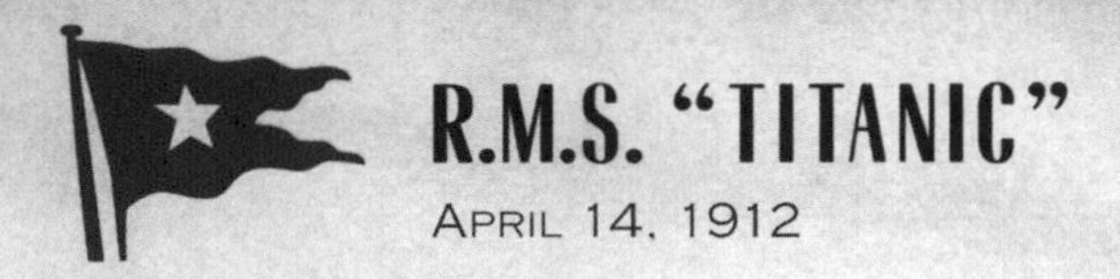

R.M.S. "TITANIC"

April 14, 1912

FIRST CLASS DINNER

Hors d'oeuvre Varies

Oysters

Consomme Olga Cream of Barley

Salmon, Mousseline Sauce, Cucumber

Filet Mignons Lili

Saute of Chicken Lyonnaise

Vegetable Marrow Farcie

Lamb, Mint Sauce

Roast Duckling, Apple Sauce

Sirloin of Beef Chateau Potatoes

Green Peas Creamed Carrots

Boiled Rice

Parmentier & Boiled New Potatoes

Punch Romaine

Roast Squab & Cress

Red Burgundy

Cold Asparagus Vinaigrette

Pate de Foie Gras

Celery

Waldorf Pudding

Peaches in Chartreuse Jelly

Chocolate & Vanilla Eclairs

French Ice Cream

for the lower decks included 'cabin biscuits' – a euphemism for hard tack. This almost indestructible mixture of flour, water, salt and a little fat, which can be stored for months, even years, had been a seafarer's staple since the Crusades. Meanwhile, in the first-class dining room, oysters were available. To offer diners these dangerously perishable bivalves four days into a voyage was possible only because of the ship's massive built-in refrigeration and ice-making units. These machines cooled separate storage rooms for mutton, beef, cheese, fish, game, mineral water, champagne and even flowers, with each room chilled to the perfect temperature for its contents. Ironically, the *Titanic* also boasted a high-capacity cooling unit, specifically for the production of ice.

Today, restaurants and dining clubs around the world, even several ocean liners, offer *Titanic*-obsessed diners the chance to taste reproductions of the first-class dining experience (no one seems to be reproducing the third-class menu). But if you really want an original menu all to yourself, you might have to spend more than you would on a first-class round-the-world cruise. In November 2015, a menu from the first-class salon sold in Dallas, Texas, for $118,750.

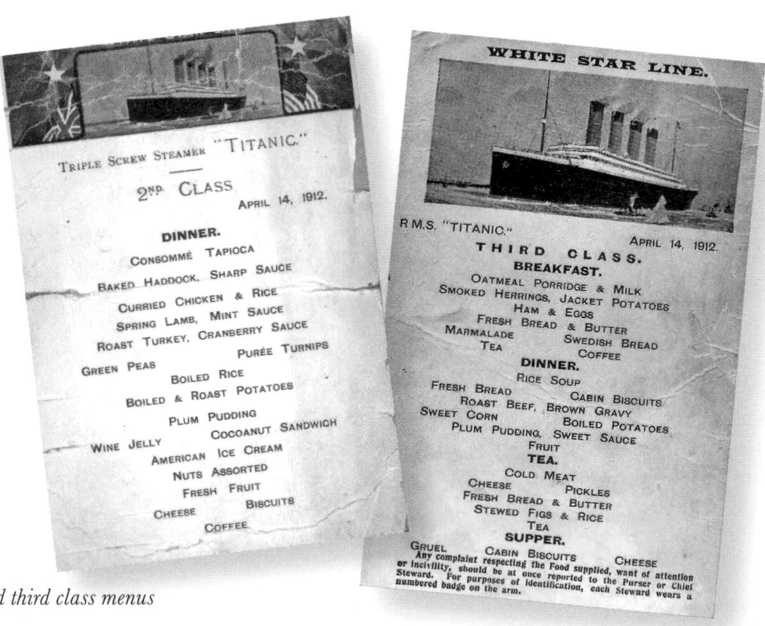

TRIPLE SCREW STEAMER "TITANIC."

2ND CLASS

APRIL 14, 1912.

DINNER.

CONSOMMÉ TAPIOCA
BAKED HADDOCK, SHARP SAUCE
CURRIED CHICKEN & RICE
SPRING LAMB, MINT SAUCE
ROAST TURKEY, CRANBERRY SAUCE
GREEN PEAS PURÉE TURNIPS
BOILED RICE
BOILED & ROAST POTATOES
PLUM PUDDING
WINE JELLY COCOANUT SANDWICH
AMERICAN ICE CREAM
NUTS ASSORTED
FRESH FRUIT
CHEESE BISCUITS
COFFEE

WHITE STAR LINE.

R.M.S. "TITANIC." APRIL 14, 1912.

THIRD CLASS.

BREAKFAST.

OATMEAL PORRIDGE & MILK
SMOKED HERRINGS, JACKET POTATOES
HAM & EGGS
FRESH BREAD & BUTTER
MARMALADE SWEDISH BREAD
TEA COFFEE

DINNER.

RICE SOUP
FRESH BREAD CABIN BISCUITS
ROAST BEEF, BROWN GRAVY
SWEET CORN BOILED POTATOES
PLUM PUDDING, SWEET SAUCE
FRUIT

TEA.

COLD MEAT
CHEESE PICKLES
FRESH BREAD & BUTTER
STEWED FIGS & RICE
TEA

SUPPER.

GRUEL CABIN BISCUITS CHEESE

Any complaint respecting the Food supplied, want of attention or incivility, should be at once reported to the Purser or Chief Steward. For purposes of identification, each Steward wears a numbered badge on the arm.

Second and third class menus

THE *HINDENBURG*'S 'MILLIONAIRE'S FLIGHT'

9 October 1936

IN OCTOBER 1936, THE GERMAN AIRSHIP *HINDENBURG* COMPLETED ITS FIRST season of transatlantic flights. To celebrate, its owners, the Zeppelin Airline Company, flew 72 wealthy and influential passengers on a ten-and-a-half-hour pleasure cruise over the autumn splendour of New England. The most powerful figures in American industry and commerce were on board, including Winthrop W. Aldrich and Nelson Rockefeller. Their combined wealth was estimated at over a billion dollars.

The menu was prepared by chef Xavier Maier, who had cooked on the smaller Graf Zepplins and had previously been head chef at the Ritz in Paris. It presents Germany's cold Rhine salmon, its Piesporter and Stein Brut wines alongside Indian swallow nest soup, California melon and Turkish coffee. It's not unusual for a menu to include dishes from around the world, but it is unusual to name each country like this. The menu, like the Hindenburg itself, is gently slipping re-energised Germany back onto the world map.

The dishes were relatively simple and demanded only a limited amount of cooking time. This was helpful in a galley that had to be powered entirely by electricity. Naked flames of any sort were banned because of the huge volume of highly flammable hydrogen that sat just above them. The only room on board in which naked flames were allowed was the smoking room, made safe by the use of a double-door airlock.

For the transatlantic journeys, the ship had to carry extra supplies, just in case storms caused delays. This was irksome in a craft where every extra ounce made it harder to get the ship aloft. Weight was such an issue that an aluminium piano was built for the bar, just to shave a few pounds off the payload.

The entire *Hindenburg* project was about re-establishing Germany's place in the world and demonstrating its newfound confidence and ambition. Which is why the company received considerable financial support from Germany's

MENU

Indian swallow nest soup

Cold Rhine salmon, spice sauce

Potato salad

1934 er Piesporter Goldtröpfchen
*(Growth G. Kirch, Cellars Poranigra
Trier-on-Moselle)*

Tenderloin Steak, Goose Liver Sauce

Chateau Potatoes

Beans à la Princesse

In Butter

1928 Feist Brut

Carmen Salad

Iced California Melon

Turkish Coffee Cakes

Liköre

Hindenburg, 1936

Propaganda Minister, Joseph Goebbels. He realised that the *Hindenburg's* real value wasn't in delivering passengers, but in delivering a message. It was a flying advertisement for the Third Reich.

Thousands of people swarmed out of factories and schools to see the *Hindenburg* take its celebratory tour. And on the tail fin of this 240m-long advertising hoarding were two swastikas, so onlookers were left in no doubt where it came from. For those who couldn't get to see it, the menu tells us that the NBC network made live radio broadcasts from on board during the flight.

By 1936, many people in the United States were becoming uncomfortable with political developments in Germany. But the *Hindenburg* was working hard to counter these misgivings. *The New York Times* wrote, 'All may not be morally well with the world, but it is not a world utterly lost when a *Hindenburg* can be built and navigated with such dramatic success.' Goebbels' blimp was working.

The day after the New England pleasure cruise, the *Hindenburg* returned to Germany, in what would be its last successful crossing. When the transatlantic service resumed the following year, as the first flight arrived in Lakehurst, New Jersey, on 7 May 1937, it burst into flames, killing 36 people and bringing lighter-than-air travel to an abrupt end.

HILLARY AND TENZING'S EVEREST MENU

29 May 1953

MENU

Sardines

Biscuits

Tinned apricots

Dates

Jam

Honey

Hot water with lemon

Mint cake

FOOD'S A BIT OF A PROBLEM ON EVEREST. THE FREEZING TEMPERATURES AND dry air make it difficult to taste anything. The lack of oxygen forces your body to concentrate on running the essentials – your brain, heart and lungs – rather than your stomach and intestines. As a result, nearly everything tastes terrible and gives you indigestion.

In 1996, Sir Edmund Hillary was asked by students what he'd eaten on his Everest-conquering expedition. He replied, 'High on the mountain, food is repugnant and you have to make yourself eat. Most of our energy came from very sweet drinks – mostly hot weak tea with lots of sugar.'

Unlike Captain Scott, who probably chose the wrong provisions for crossing the Antarctic (see page 16), Colonel John Hunt, who was in charge of the Everest expedition, seems to have got it right. It's all about easily digestible foods – sugars and carbohydrates that are quickly converted into energy. And it's about strong tastes that are likely to appeal to climbers when freezing temperatures have dulled their senses. So sardines and mint cake may be just the ticket. Even people who find the intense sweetness of mint cake disgusting when it's 12°C and they're standing at sea level may find it delicious at 8,800m when it's –26°C.

When Romney's, the manufacturers of mint cake, were asked to provide the 1953 Everest expedition with 36lb (over 16kg) of the stuff – the weight one Sherpa can carry – they faced a problem. As sugar was still rationed in Britain, they had to get permission from the Ministry of Food before they could supply Hunt's men with such a large amount. Some sources suggest that workers at the Romney's factory donated their own food coupons to help make up the order.

While most of us know to drink lots when it's hot, dehydration is also a real problem for climbers in extreme cold. So they need to consume vast quantities of tea, brewed from melting snow. However, the reduced atmospheric pressure at the summit of Everest means water boils at about 71°C, so the quality of the tea may be questionable even after spoonfuls of sugar have been added.

As well as consuming food on Everest, Sherpa Tenzing Norgay, who accompanied Hillary to the summit, also left some behind, digging a small hole and burying sweets and chocolate as a Buddhist offering. Although this did little to mar the unspoilt beauty of the world's highest peak, the thousands of climbers who have come after him have turned Everest into Earth's highest rubbish dump. Food containers, camping equipment, oxygen cylinders and human faeces all contribute to what some environmentalists estimate to be more than 100 tonnes of waste. To help deal with the problem, since 2014, Sherpas have been paid two dollars for each kilo of rubbish they bring down the mountain. ◈

Kendal Mint Cake

MENU

Four bacon squares

Peaches

Three sugar cookies

Pineapple-grapefruit drink

Coffee

THE FIRST MENU ON THE MOON

20 July 1969

THERE ARE LOTS OF 'FIRST FOODS IN SPACE'. YURI GAGARIN WAS THE FIRST human to eat in space, enjoying tasty beef and liver paste squeezed out of a tube in 1961. The following year John Glenn feasted on some apple sauce and scrumptious xylose sugar tablets. The first solid food eaten was smuggled on board Gemini 3 by pilot John Young. It was a corned-beef sandwich on rye and was actually not a smart move since crumbs from the bread could have damaged the spacecraft's electronic systems.

But the first menu eaten by astronauts on the moon is the one opposite. There were three main meals on rotation – A, B, and C – and the historic first one was not specially planned; at a slightly different time the menu could just as easily have featured tuna salad, butterscotch pudding or chicken stew. Neil Armstrong's personal favourite, according to James Hansen's biography *First Man: The Life of Neil A. Armstrong*, was Meal C on the Day 2 rota – spaghetti with meat sauce, pork and scalloped potatoes, pineapple fruitcake and grape punch. Armstrong's colleague Buzz Aldrin preferred the shrimp cocktail.

Bacon had been a popular choice since the first manned Apollo mission and featured heavily in the crew's meal choices. Though it's a less common choice today, British astronaut Tim Peake's first meal in space in 2015 on board the International Space Station was a bacon sandwich.

But was this really the first moon food? In fact, Buzz Aldrin privately took communion before Meal A, eating a wafer and sipping communion wine before anybody sampled the bacon. An elder at his Presbyterian church in Texas, Aldrin then read from the Gospel of John 15:5. 'I am the vine, you are the branches. Whoever abides in me will bring forth much fruit. Apart from me you can do nothing.' ◈

CONCORDE'S RECORD ROUND-THE-WORLD FLIGHT

1995

THERE'S SOMETHING VERY FAMILIAR ABOUT THE FIRST IN-FLIGHT AIRLINE food supplied by Handley Page Transport in 1919. For the princely sum of three shillings, passengers flying from Hounslow Heath in London to Le Bourget in Paris could buy a pre-packed lunch box containing a sandwich, a piece of fruit and some chocolate.

Airline food really took off in 1936 when United Airlines pioneered the first onboard kitchens, now long since gone, which provided passengers with hot meals during flights. Caterers today search endlessly for ways to make their menus tempting, from cutting up food in the shape of the Hello Kitty icon (Taiwan's EVA Air) to serving KFC over Christmas (Japan Airlines). And of course bosses have their own take on how the meals should look – legend has it that the former Chief Executive of American Airlines, Robert Crandall, lopped $40,000 off the company's food outgoings by taking out a single olive from each salad served to passengers in first class.

The odds are certainly stacked against the cooks. For a start, high-quality mass catering is not easy. Singapore Airlines, for example, serves about 50,000 meals a day. Reheating pre-prepared meals

MENU

Canapés – Champagne

Lobster salad with a julienne of mango and pear

Tournedos in peppercorn sauce

Potato croquette with truffles and slivered almonds, carrot and spinach subric

Seasonal salad

Cheese from France

Fresh fruit salad

Petits fours

cooked on the ground for this many people is never going to improve flavours.

Moreover, a mixture of pressurisation and constant aeroplane engine noise tends to make food taste dry and flavourless as taste buds struggle to detect anything sweet or salty. Poor humidity dries out the nose, which also reduces tasting sensation – Heston Blumenthal's cunning plan to deal with this issue for British Airways passengers was to provide everybody with an individual nasal spray. Meanwhile, on its Dreamliner 14,498km Perth–London direct service, Qantas offers a 'jet-lag menu'. Among various dishes designed to aid relaxation or sleep, there is an emphasis on ingredients to help with hydration, including green leafy vegetables, cucumber, strawberries and celery.

The result is that over the years airline menus have come in for plenty of stick, not least from celebrity chef Gordon Ramsay, who once commented in his usual pithy style that 'There's no f*****g way I eat on planes.' It's also telling that cabin crews tend to bring their own food to work.

In contrast, Concorde's catering was lavish from the start and even inspired its own dish, the luscious Gateau Concorde, with layers of chocolate meringue and chocolate mousse. The offering featured opposite comes from the eastbound New York–Toulouse section of the flight during which the Air France Concorde circumnavigated the planet in 31 hours, 27 minutes and 49 seconds. It certainly stands comparison with its maiden passenger flight in 1976, when leading French chef Paul Bocuse created a menu which featured caviar and lobster canapés, fillet steak, Dom Perignon 1969 champagne and Havana cigars (smoking was not banned on Concorde until 1997). Michel Roux and Richard Corrigan were among later famous chefs who devised Concorde's weekly-changing menus.

The food was marvellous to the very end. When the likes of Joan Collins and Sir David Frost boarded the final flight on 24 October 2003, they were treated to lobster fishcakes with Bloody Mary relish and wilted spinach, Scottish smoked salmon with caviar, pancetta-wrapped prime fillet of beef, lamb cutlet, wild mushroom and truffle omelette with hash browns and grilled tomato, and a choice of three champagnes – including Pol Roger Cuvée Sir Winston Churchill, 1986 – all listed on a lovely silver-grey menu card with double grey tassle.

INTERNATIONAL SPACE STATION EXPEDITION 1'S MENU

November 2000–March 2001

On 12 April 1961, Yuri Gagarin became the first man in space. He beat the USA's Alan Shepard to the title by about three weeks. Not until 20 July 1969, when Neil Armstrong took one small step on the Moon, was American pride restored. The Space Race was the Cold War played out over our heads in a contest that cost both sides billions of dollars.

But after glasnost and the fall of the Berlin Wall, the two superpowers came together to build the embodiment of the new world order. In November 1998, a rocket carrying the first of 40 components that would make up the International Space Station was launched – and with it, a whole new era of space dining.

This menu for Expedition 1 reflects the new atmosphere of co-operation and cohabitation. Borscht and beef stroganoff sit side by side with macaroni cheese and brownies. This six-day cycle of four meals a day would feed the three-man crew for 136 days. But even 500km above the Earth, some things are just the same as they are down here: who takes their coffee with or without sugar is noted, to make sure no one gets upset with the wrong beverage. The meals are divided into traditional patterns – breakfast through to supper. When your home orbits the Earth every hour and a half, you can't rely on the sun to set your body clock, so routines like this help to maintain

A close-up view of a food tray scheduled to be used in the Skylab programme.

the crew's mental and physical health.

As with all travel food, the technology available to preserve it plays a big part in shaping the menu. On the ISS, food comes in five forms:

1: THERMOSTABILISED – *e.g. cooked tuna or grilled chicken, sealed in a pouch or tin.*

2: DEHYDRATED – *e.g. dried mashed potato or spaghetti, to be mixed with boiling water.*

3: IRRADIATED – *in this case, beef steaks that have been exposed to radiation to kill bacteria.*

4: INTERMEDIATE MOISTURE – *e.g. dried apricots or bread, with limited water and a long shelf life.*

5: NATURAL FORM – *e.g. cookies or peanut butter, which are just the same as at home.*

Although the regular menu lacks fresh fruit and vegetables, rockets bringing new supplies or new crew members often deliver fresh produce too. As there's no refrigeration on board, these have to be eaten fairly quickly. This lack of refrigeration also means that cold drinks are never any cooler than lukewarm.

There are fewer dehydrated dishes than on earlier mission menus due to how the ISS is powered. Rocket and shuttle missions were powered by fuel cells that produced water as a by-product, which was used to re-hydrate the food. But the ISS is powered by solar panels, so water must be recycled from the atmosphere.

If the crew doesn't like the food – despite taste-testing it before launch and choosing their preferred meals – they can add condiments. Chilli sauce is especially popular. This is because, in zero gravity, fluids in the body don't drain as they do on Earth. As a result, crew members often complain of feeling congested. And as anyone with a head cold will tell you, this makes food taste bland. Salt and pepper can't be sprinkled, though. Without gravity, they're just as likely to drift off into a control panel as they are to flavour your food. Instead, astronauts spread salt and pepper paste. For the same reason, flatbreads are preferred to their crumblier counterparts. They also pack more calories and have a longer shelf life than traditional loaves.

The ISS appears to be a celebration of unity and co-operation. In fact, the Western and Russian crews are mostly separated. They work and sleep in different areas, carrying out research and experiments that are rarely shared. As is so often the case, it's meals that bring people together. Although they have their own food, prepared and delivered by their own teams on Earth, they eat together, swapping canned Russian fish for American pastries, granola bars for cottage cheese.

Day 1

MEAL 1

Cottage Cheese w/ Nuts (R)
Plum-Cherry Dessert (IM)
Russkoye Cookies (NF)
Tea w/o Sugar

MEAL 2

Seasoned Scrambled Eggs (R)
Sausage Pattie (R)
Oatmeal w/ Raisins & Spice (R)
Waffle (T)
Orange-Grapefruit Drink (B)
Coffee Black (B)

MEAL 3

Puréed Vegetable Soup (R)
Chicken w/ Rice (T)
Moscow Rye Bread (IM)
Apple-Peach Juice w/ Pulp (R)

MEAL 4

Turkey Tetrazzini (R)
Tomatoes & Eggplant (T)
Shortbread Cookies (NF)
Fruit Cocktail (T)
Tropical Punch (B)

Day 2

MEAL 1

Chicken w/ Prunes (T)
Buckwheat Gruel (R) – Shep & Gidzenko
Buckwheat Gruel w /Milk (R) – Krikalev
Vostok Cookies (NF)
Coffee w/o Sugar (R) – Krikalev
Cow Milk (R) – Shephard
Apricot Juice w/ Pulp (R) – Gidzenko

MEAL 2

Tuna Salad Spread (T)
Macaroni & Cheese (R)
Crackers (NF)
Green Beans w/ Mushrooms (T)
Lemonade (B)

MEAL 3

Kharcho Mutton Soup (R) – Shep & Gidzenko
Puréed Vegetable Soup (R) – Krikalev
Beef w/ Vegetables (R)
Borodinskly Bread (IM) – Kirkalev
Table Bread (IM) – Shep & Gidzenko
Peach-Blackcurrant Juice w/ Pulp (R)
Tea w/ Sugar

MEAL 4

Ham (T)
Potatoes au Gratin (R)
Shortbread Cookies (NF)
Pears (T)
Orange-Grapefruit Drink (B)

Day 3

MEAL 1

Cottage Cheese w/ Nuts (R)
Plum-Cherry Dessert (IM)
Coffee w/Sugar (R)

MEAL 2

Grilled Chicken (T)
Rice w/ Butter (T)
Creamed Spinach (R)
Pineapple (T)
Grapefruit Drink (B)

MEAL 3

Borscht w/ Meat (R)
Meat w/ Vermicelli (T) – Shep & Gidzenko
Meat w/ Buckwheat Gruel (R) – Krikalev
Borodinsky Bread (IM)
Hazelnuts (NF)
Tea w/ Sugar (R)
Apple-Blackcurrant Juice w/ Pulp (R)

MEAL 4

Beef Stroganoff w/ Noodles
Dinner Roll (NF)
Butter Cookies (NF)
Orange-Mango Drink (B)

(B) Beverage
(R) Rehydrate
(IM) Intermediate Moisture
(T) Thermostabilized
(I) Irradiated
(T) Natural Form

Day 4

MEAL 1

Rossiyskiy Cheese (T)
Honey Cake (IM)
Apple-Plum Bar (IM)
Coffee w/ Sugar – Krikalev & Gidzenko

MEAL 2

Beef Pattie (R)
Cauliflower w/ Cheese (R)
Chocolate Pudding (T)
Orange-Pineapple Drink (B)
Kona Coffee Black (B)

MEAL 3

Peasant Soup (R)
Beef Goulash (T)
Mashed Potatoes w/ Onions (R)
Moscow Rye Bread (R)
Tea w/ Sugar (R)
Peach-Apricot Juice w/ Pulp

MEAL 4

Teriyaki Chicken (R)
Rice & Chicken (R)
Peaches (T)
Almonds (NF)
Pineapple Drink (B)

Day 5

MEAL 1

Cottage Cheese/Nuts (R)
Honey Cake (IM)
Kuraga (IM)
Vostok Cookies (NF)
Coffee w/o Sugar (R) – Shephard
Coffee w/ Sugar (R) – Krikalev & Gidzenko

MEAL 2

Spaghetti w/ Meat Sauce (R)
Broccoli au Gratin (R)
Brownie (NF)
Pineapple Drink (B)
Vanilla Breakfast Drink (B)

MEAL 3

Pickled Cucumber/Meat Soup (R)
Pork w/ Potatoes (T)
Borodinsky Bread (IM)
Grape-Plum Juice w/ Pulp (R)
Tea w/Sugar

MEAL 4

Smoked Turkey (I)
Italian Vegetables (R)
Strawberries (R)
Granola Bar (NF)
Grape Drink (B)

Day 6

MEAL 1

Oatmeal w/ Chicken (T)
Sweet Peas w/ Milk Sauce (R)
Prunes Stuffed w/ Nuts (IM)
Russkoye Cookies (NF)
Tea w/ Sugar (R)

MEAL 2

Grilled Chicken (T)
Rice w/Butter (T)
Creamed Spinach (R)
Pineapple (T)
Grapefruit Drink (B)

MEAL 3

Sauerkraut Soup (R) – Shepherd
Meat w/ Barley Kasha (T) – Shepherd
Pureed Vegetable Soup (R) – Krikalev
Chicken in White Sauce (T) – Krikalev
Bream in Tomato Sauce (T) – Krikalev
Mashed Potatoes (R) – Gidzenko
Moscow Rye Bread (IM)
Apricot Juice w/ Pulp (R)

MEAL 4

Shrimp Cocktail (R)
Beef Steak (I)
Corn (R)
Apple Sauce (T)
Orange Drink (B)

CHAPTER TWO

CAFÉS AND RESTAURANTS

Our country-hopping tour includes a little Lyon's Corner House nostalgia, a groundbreaking feminist lunch in New York, the world's first vegetarian restaurant in Switzerland, and the farewell magic of elBulli in Spain.

BRITAIN'S FIRST INDIAN RESTAURANT

1810

There are an estimated 30,000 curry restaurants in Britain. They're the nation's favourite choice for a meal out. It's often assumed that the first of them appeared in the 1960s or '70s. But it's way back in 1810 that Sake Dean Mahomed opened the doors to Britain's first Indian restaurant, the Hindoostane Dinner and Hooka Smoking Club in Marylebone.

His menu combined Indian spices with popular ingredients of the time – lobster, veal and pineapples (see page 66 for more about the Georgians' love of pineapples). The use of these fashionable ingredients was important. This restaurant wasn't catering for Indian sailors passing through London's port. It was for middle-class English diners. And it wasn't cheap. The pineapple pullaoo cost the equivalent of £122 in today's money. Even a coolmah of lamb would set diners back the equivalent of around £30.

Curry was already popular in Britain when Mahomed opened his restaurant. Hannah Glasse's *The Art Of Cookery Made Plain and Simple*, published in 1747, contains recipes for both curries and pilaus. But these were mild recipes, flavoured with coriander, pepper, herbs and lemon juice. It was only later, after the British East India Company had placed India at the heart of the Empire, that caraway, fenugreek, ginger and cumin became popular. Mahomed set out to

MENU

Makee Pullaoo	*£1.1.0*
Pineapple Pullaoo	*£1.16.0*
Chicken Pullaoo	*£1.1.0*
Lamb Pullaoo	*£1.1.0*
Chicken Curry	*£0.12.0*
Lobster Curry	*£0.12.0*
Coolmah of Lamb or Veal	*£0.8.0*

TOGETHER WITH BREADS, CHUTNEYS AND OTHER EXCLUSIVELY INDIAN DISHES

capitalise on this growing taste for spicy foods.

He took out large advertisements in *The Times*, informing customers that 'such ladies and gentleman as may be desirous of having India Dinners dressed and sent to their own houses will be punctually attended to...' In other words, his restaurant was also the country's first Indian takeaway.

Mahomed was born in Bengal in 1759. He joined the army of the British East India Company as a trainee surgeon and rose to the rank of captain. He resigned in 1782, moved to Cork and met Jane Daly. They eloped, married and eventually settled in London. It was here that Mahomed saw the growing demand for Indian food from former employees of the British East India Company. Sadly, after two years, the restaurant failed. He was declared bankrupt and had to move to Brighton, where he offered his services as a butler and valet. Mahomed would rise again, though, becoming the 'shampooing surgeon' to both George IV and William IV.

We're very lucky to know what was on Mahomed's menu at all. Printed menus were rare in Georgian Britain. This is a handwritten list of 25 dishes – all with their prices – that was found inside a notebook. The writer admits that the list isn't complete, concluding that there were 'various other dishes too numerous for insertion'. Complete or not, the book containing this rare menu was auctioned in June 2018 for over £8,500. ◈

CITY OF WESTMINSTER
SITE OF
HINDOOSTANE
COFFEE HOUSE
1810
LONDON'S FIRST
INDIAN RESTAURANT.
OWNED BY
SAKE DEAN MAHOMED
1759-1851
THE PORTMAN ESTATE

Above: Sake Dean Mahomed.

CHICKEN PILAU WITH RAITA

SERVES 6

For the marinade

½ teaspoon turmeric
½ teaspoon red chilli powder
2 teaspoon ground cumin
2 teaspoon ground coriander
4 tablespoons natural yoghurt
1 teaspoon salt
500g (17½oz) diced chicken breast

For the Pilau

8 cashew nuts
2 teaspoon poppy seeds
3 tablespoons vegetable oil
2 white onions, peeled and sliced
2 tablespoons ghee or clarified butter (optional)
1 cinnamon stick
5 cardamom pods, crushed
4 cloves
2 blades of mace
2 bay leaves
1 inch of ginger, peeled and grated
3 garlic cloves, peeled and grated
2 green chillies, sliced
300g (10½oz) soaked basmati rice
salt and a pinch of sugar

For the Raita

250g (9oz) natural yoghurt
½ cucumber, peeled, de-seeded and finally chopped
pinch of salt

Make the marinade by combining all the spices, yoghurt and salt together and then adding in the diced chicken. Cover and place in the fridge.

Using a pestle and mortar, make a paste of the cashew nuts and the poppy seeds. Use a tablespoon of water to help get a smooth paste. Leave this to one side.

Heat the vegetable oil in a heavy-based casserole pan which has a tight-fitting lid. Add the sliced onions and cook for 8-10 minutes on a medium heat until they start to brown. Remove them from the pan and set aside.

Add the ghee (or you can use vegetable oil again) to the warm pan and fry all the whole spices and the bay leaves for 2-3 minutes before adding the grated ginger, garlic and chilli. Cook for a further 1-2 minutes with a tablespoon of water.

Add the cashew and poppy seed paste followed by the marinated chicken. Fry for 5 minutes on a medium heat until the chicken starts to colour. If you notice the paste is burning, add 1 tablespoon water and reduce the heat. Season with salt at this stage.

Add the soaked rice and 550ml water. Bring to a simmer and cover with a tight-fitting lid. Cook the Pilau for 20 minutes until all the water has been absorbed and the rice is perfectly cooked.

While the pilau is cooking, combine the yoghurt with the chopped cucumber and salt to the raita.

Serve the pilau while hot with the raita on the side.

THE FRIED FISH SHOP.

FISH AND CHIPS

1863 to the Present Day

WE MIGHT THINK THE GREAT DOUBLE ACT FISH AND CHIPS IS AS BRITISH as Torvill and Dean, Morecambe and Wise or wind and rain. But in fact it was Jewish refugees from Portugal and Spain, arriving in the seventeenth century, who introduced Britain to the street food that would become their national dish – fish fried in flour. It was French and Belgian Huguenots, coming shortly afterwards, who introduced fried potatoes in the form of frites. What the British did was bring the two together. And what led to the duo becoming a legend was the Industrial Revolution.

By the middle of the nineteenth century, the population of Britain's cities had exploded. Work was no longer centred around the home, but around a factory, with every member of the family employed there. There was often no one at home to prepare food for the end of the working day. The result was a need for cheap, hot food that could be sold in large quantities to entire shifts of workers as they left their mills and factories. And as a girl born in 1841 was not expected to live to see her 43rd birthday, the salt and fat content of that food didn't really matter.

If the Industrial Revolution made fish and chips desirable, it also made them possible. The new trawling methods and steam-powered vessels made cod, hake and haddock affordable in vast quantities. And the railways allowed fresh fish to be transported to the industrial towns of the Midlands and the North. Haddock was the favoured fish in the North-east, hake in the North-west, rock salmon in the South and cod everywhere.

MENU

Fish
(cod, haddock, hake or rock salmon)

Chips

Fish cakes

Mushy peas

Curry sauce

Who gets the credit for opening the first fish and chip shop is a question that lies at the heart of the North/South divide. Londoners will tell you that Joseph Malin, whose shop in the East End opened in 1860, takes the title. Northerners will point to John Lees's shop in Mossley, near Oldham. Whoever was first, by 1930 they had over 35,000 competitors across the country.

Fish and chips became such an important part of British culture that wartime governments felt it was too important for morale to be rationed. But that didn't mean fish was always available, and the war years saw the introduction of the fish cake – an often microscopic portion of fish sandwiched between two slices of potato, dipped in batter and fried. Bryan's fish shop in Leeds served these with the warning, 'Patrons: We do not recommend the use of vinegar with these fish cakes.'

The only vegetable on the standard fish-and-chip menu is mushy peas – dried marrowfat peas, soaked overnight and then cooked with bicarbonate of soda and salt. Loved and loathed in equal measure, they're the perfect industrial dish. The peas aren't fresh, so they don't go off, which reduces waste and therefore cost. They're dried, so they're cheap to transport. And there's no seasonal variation or change in quality – like all good industrial processes, peas can be mushed cheaply and consistently every day of the year.

Fish and chip shop illustration, circa 1900.

HOT FISH & CHIPS
HOT FISH & CHIPS

Migrants introduced Britain to fish and chips in the eighteenth and nineteenth century. In the 20th century, new arrivals, this time from southern Asia, moved the menu on, offering curry sauce as a moist alternative to mushy peas. But these new arrivals also brought other dishes to tempt the takeaway diner – bhajis, bhunas and biryanis. The popularity of American culture following World War ll saw the arrival of the burger joint and the fried-chicken shop. Fish and chips were losing their dominance of Friday nights.

Kate Winslet may have served them at her wedding, and many people still don't think they've been to the seaside unless they've eaten them with a wooden fork, but the popularity of fish and chips has waned since its heyday in the 1930s. There are now just 10,500 chip shops left in captivity, and curry has replaced fish and chips as the most popular takeaway in the UK. ◈

Caledonian Market, London, circa 1935

Menu

Huîtres

Potages

Tortue verte
Consommé Souveraine

Hors d'oeuvre

Radis Olives Céleri

Poisson

Truites à la meunière
Pommes de terre, Laurette
Concombres

Relevé

Selle d'agneau, sauce Colbert
Céleri braisé

Entrées

Terrapène à la Maryland

Asperges nouvelles, sauce Hollandaise

Sorbet au kirsch

Rôts

Pluviers
Salade chiffonade

Entremets de douceur

Coupole St. Charles
Gâteaux
Fromage
Café

Lundi, 3 Avril, 1899
DELMONICOS

FIRST LADIES' LUNCHEON

Delmonico's, New York, 1868

THE FOOD ON THIS 1899 MENU – HEAVY ON TURTLE (BOTH AS SOUP AND IN sauce) – is almost entirely irrelevant. Its interest lies in the fact that it is the earliest printed Ladies' Luncheon menu in the archives of the New York Public Library and represents the growing liberation of women in the USA.

Three decades earlier, on 18 April 1868, Delmonico's in New York, then arguably the country's most famous restaurant, played host to a dinner honouring Charles Dickens, who was on a reading tour of the USA (see page 166). It was organised by the New York Press Club and no women were invited. Indeed, at this time restaurants did not allow women to dine without a male at their side.

Reporter Jane Cunningham Croly was having none of it. She complained to the Press Club. Grudgingly it relented and said that she and other female journalists could attend after all. So long as they ate hidden behind a curtain. Croly – who wrote under the pen name Jennie June and campaigned for better working conditions for women – declined their offer.

Two days later, Croly and a dozen women entered Delmonico's. These were middle- and upper-class women, they all worked, and this was the first meeting of what became the first American professional women's association, Sorosis (a botanical term for fruits made from the ovaries of several flowers). They spoke to the restaurant's owner, Lorenzo Delmonico, and explained that they would like to eat lunch without a man at their table. He agreed and history was made, Delmonico's becoming the official meeting place for the club.

Sorosis grew to nearly a hundred members by the end of the year and helped to launch similar women's clubs around the country, although other restaurants were less progressive and some kept the male-chaperone rule in place into the 1960s. A ban on men and women who are not married or closely related eating together is still enforced in some parts of the world, such as certain provinces of Indonesia, today. ◈

Poster for Haus Hiltl restaurant, Zurich.

FIRST VEGETARIAN RESTAURANT

Haus Hiltl, Zurich, 1898

Although it has always been possible to avoid devouring animals when going out to eat, the *Guinness World Records* categorically states that the world's oldest vegetarian restaurant is Haus Hiltl, founded on 3 July 1898 in Zurich, Switzerland. The menu overleaf is from the year it opened its doors, when it was called Vegetarierheim und Abstinenz Café.

Bavarian-born Ambrosius Hiltl took over the restaurant six years later at a time when the notion of a vegetarian diet was regarded as rather odd, and a specialised restaurant even more so. This was something of a career change for Hiltl, who had previously been a tailor, but he was impressed with the concept of a vegetarian diet and credited his recovery from rheumatism to the meat-free regime developed for him by the man who made muesli famous, Swiss nutritionist Maximilian Bircher-Benner.

Ambrosius eventually handed control to his sons Walter and Leonard, and it was Leonard's wife Margrith who returned from the World Vegetarian Congress in Delhi in 1951 with plans for adding elements of Indian cooking to the menu. After further success and expansion, the restaurant is now run by fourth-generation family member Rolf Hiltl under the umbrella Hiltl name. There are currently seven Hiltls around the city and the expansion includes the Hiltl Academy which offers cookery courses and kitchen parties, as well as the country's first vegetarian butchery.

The earliest menu available for Hiltl dates from 12 October 1898 and started with a soup of the day, followed by salads (cucumber, mixed, and with eggs), and then an assortment of vegetables (sprouts, braised white cabbage, spinach with egg, carrots with peas, cauliflower in butter sauce, baked cauliflower with salad, potatoes with butter, potatoes with sour milk, and roast potatoes).

Moving on to the grains section (*Mehlspeisen*), diners could enjoy porridge in milk with fruit, fried rice, fruity bread and butter pudding, or fried macaroni.

Alkoholhaltige Getränke werden nicht verabreicht.

„Vegetarierheim"

Vegetarisches Speisehaus Abstinenz-Café

Speise-Karte.

Zürich, den 6. November 1898.

Suppe:

Kraftbrühe m. Einlage	15

Körner- und Hülsenfrüchte:

Weisse Bohnen	15

Salate

Kopfsalat (mit Ei 35)	20
Karottensalat	20
Rettichsalat	20
Gemischten Salat	20
Rosenkohl	25

Gemüse:

Kohlrabi	25
Gemüse allerlei	35
Spinat (mit Ei 40)	25
Carfiol gebacken	35
mit Salat	55
Butterreis	20
Kartoffelstock	10

Mehlspeisen:

Gries in Milch	20
mit Obst	25
Strudel gefüllt	25
Gugelhopf	25
Äpfel im Schlafrock	15

Obst und Kompots:

Zwetschgen	15
Äpfel	20
Gemischtes	25

Verschiedenes:

Himbeeren	20
Grahambrot 1 Stück	05
Äpfelsaft per Glas	10
Limonade " "	10
Milch	10
Milchkaffee Tasse	10
Schwarztee, Kräutertee	10

Members of the Vegetarierheim und Abstinenz Café.

To end, there were damsons, elderberries, apples, raspberries, pear jam, plums and grapes. All prices are in 'rappen', the Swiss currency of the day.

Even if your German is decent, you may be disconcerted by some of the spellings, since some words in 19th-century German were spelt with a 'c' where today a 'k' is used, for example '*carfiol*' instead of '*karfiol*' (cauliflower), four lines from the bottom of column one, under the heading 'Gemüse'.

Today, the restaurant's menu has changed somewhat, and dishes include the signature Hiltl Tatar (okra, aubergine/eggplant and spices), soy chocolate mousse and a vegan wine list (the menu from 1898 declares that no alcohol will be served), as well as a vast hot and cold buffet.

In 2018, Switzerland topped a survey of which European countries best catered for vegetarians. Around three per cent of the population do not eat meat, and just under a fifth describe themselves as 'flexitarians', eating meat only occasionally.

BLUE PHEASANT TEA ROOM

1921–22

THE MIAMI METROPOLITAN AREA IS NOW HOME TO OVER SIX MILLION PEOPLE. But in the 1890s, 40 years before art-deco architecture began to define Miami's coastline, it was a predominantly rural landscape, populated by pioneers living in scattered homesteads.

Teacher Flora MacFarlane was concerned about the isolation that women living on these homesteads were experiencing. So in 1891 she founded the Housekeepers' Club, Florida's first ever women's organisation. Its purpose was to allow women to 'spend two hours a week in companionship and study'. But these were pioneer women, and they did much more than that.

They raised money by selling handicrafts and teas at fairs and used the profits to build Florida's first integrated church, a schoolroom, a library and then their own clubhouse. All in under ten years. By the early twentieth century, the club's members were the backbone of the conservation movement to preserve the Everglades, buying up land which developers wanted to reclaim for agriculture and proselytising about the importance of the area's wildlife.

In 1920 they built a new clubhouse, part of which housed the Blue Pheasant Tea Room, which they ran to raise more funds for their work. The original tea room's menu is crude, handwritten and backed by coconut husk. But the range of teas it offers is extraordinary – not just English Breakfast, but teas from Ceylon, Taiwan, India and Japan, even the café's own blend. It also has maté, which aficionados will tell you is not a tea but an infusion, made from a holly-like bush that's native to South America. In the years following the Boston Tea Party of 1773, when three British ships had their cargo of tea dumped into Boston harbour by the Sons of Liberty, drinking tea was seen as an unpatriotic act in the United States. This attitude helped coffee to establish its place as the king of beverages. But here in the southern States, tea has clearly made a comeback.

The menu also reflects Caribbean influences on Florida's culture. While a

Beverages

Afternoon Tea	
Cup	.15
Pot	.25

Blue Pheasant Special

Formosa Oolong – Orlof
Orange Pekoe – Ceylon
English Breakfast – Kohinoor
Sun-baked Japan – Nassac
Yerbé Mate – Paraguay
Special – Jasmine Tea,
Imported Direct

Cup	.25
Pot	.25
Cuban coffee, per cup	.25
Cocoa, per cup	.25
Cocoa, with whipped cream	.30
Malted milk, hot or iced	.25
Limeade, per glass	.25
Mint Limeade	.25
Blue Pheasant Punch	.30
Orange juice, per glass	.25
Coco de Agua	.30

Note: special arrangement may be made for luncheons and parties

Buttered Toast with Grated Cheese	.25
Cinnamon Toast	.25
Buttered Toast with Marmalade [Grape-Fruit, Orange, Kumquat, Panama Orange, Guava]	.30
Blue Pheasant Sandwhich	.30
Orange Sandwhich	.30
Nut Bread Sandwhich	.25
Cucumber Sandwhich	.25
Lettuce Sandwhich	.25
Cream Cheese Sandwhich [Olive, Nut or Pepper]	.25
Jam Sandwhich	.20
Blue Pheasant Salád	.40
Poinsettia Salad	.40
Coconut Macaroons	.25
Sponge Cakes	.25
Cake, per slice	.40

cup of coffee is now described as an americano around the world, here a cup of coffee is Cuban. And hidden among the cucumber sandwiches and sponge cakes are coconut water and guava. The rest is unremarkable, with the possible exception of poinsettia salad. This doesn't actually contain poinsettias, but is designed to look like one, so was once popular at Christmas. Lettuce leaves are topped with slices of pineapple, cream cheese and maraschino cherries, then covered in salad dressing. Few people can be sorry about its demise. ◈

McDONALD'S

1943

No Golden Arches, no Ronald, no Big Mac. The first incarnation of McDonald's was actually called The Airdrome. Situated in Monrovia, California, it sold hot dogs and orange juice – it was not until 1940, when brothers Maurice and Richard McDonald moved operations to San Bernardino, California, that the company's iconic name was first used.

At this point, it was called McDonald's Bar-B-Que, since it focused on exactly that style of food. 'We barbecue all meats in our own barbecue pit' ran its slogan, slightly more descriptive than 'I'm Lovin' It'. Barbecued beef, ham or pork (with French fries) would set you back 35 cents, the Aristocratic burger was 25 cents and you could wash it down with a Frosted Root Beer or Giant Malt (20 cents each). Eight years later and five years after the menu featured above, the brothers realised that by far their biggest moneyspinners were hamburgers, and they developed their own fast-food 'Speedee Service System' production technique to produce them as quickly as possible. They were then bought out by entrepreneur Ray Kroc, who turned the business into the vast planet-wide corporation we have today, so big indeed that *The Economist* magazine's Big Mac Index is based

MENU

Barbecued Beef, Ham or Pork with French Fries

Aristocratic Hamburgers with French Fries

Melted Cheese with French Fries

Peanut Butter and Jelly with French Fries

Hamburger Steak with French Fries

Tamales and Chilli with French Fries

Order of Straight Chilli

Ham and Baked Beans

Hamburger Royal with Chilli and Beans

on the eponymous dish's sales price in world currencies to, as they put it, 'make exchange-rate theory more digestible'.

McDonald's adjusts its menus around the world to cater for varying palates and requirements (although there are still some places, such as Iceland and most of Africa, where it has no outlets). Many in Asia serve soup, and there are various kosher branches in Israel which do not serve pork products. Filet-O-Fish was developed partly to appeal to Catholic customers during Lent and on Fridays.

This means you can experiment in Japan with the Ebi Filet-O Shrimp burger or in Malaysia with the Korean Spicy Burger which has a black bun coloured with bamboo charcoal. Meanwhile in Singapore you can enjoy fries sprinkled

1950s McDonald's restaurant.

with nori seaweed flakes. Other delights which are less widespread include:

- Bubur Ayam McD (Malaysia) – according to McDonald's this is 'juicy chicken strips in mouth-watering porridge, garnished with spring onions, sliced ginger, fried shallots and diced chilis. Just like mum's cooking!'
- Taro Pie (China) – made from a sweet purple tuber.
- McCurry Pan (India) – curried vegetables in a cream sauce inside an edible crispy bread basket.
- Chicha Purple Temptation (Peru) – a pudding made with blue corn, a variation on the country's national chicha morada drink.
- McMollette (Mexico) – a breakfast of warm bread, covered with beans, cheese and salsa.
- Poutine (Canada) – 'Rich and tasty gravy? Melty, mouth-watering cheese curds? On our World Famous Fries? You better believe it!'

Not all innovations have stood the test of time. The Hula Burger – a burger made up of a slice of pineapple and a slice of cheese – is no longer with us;

Modern McDonalds menu in Busan, South Korea.

neither is the McLean Deluxe sandwich, which was built around a 91-per-cent fat-free beefburger. The marvellously titled McNürnburger consisted of three Bratwurst in a bun with mustard and onions, but did not do well in Germany. The McHotDog was not a great success, nor the McLobster, which is essentially seasonal. Rather more seriously, the McAfrika (beef, cheese and tomato in a pitta sandwich) was released in 2002, just as many African countries were facing famine. A PR disaster, it was quickly withdrawn.

There are also intriguing legends of a 'secret menu' available at McDonald's, although this appears to consist of simply adding several options together, such as the Land, Sea and Air Burger (two beef patties, two chicken patties and a Filet-O-Fish), rather than an under-the-counter Filet-O-Badger. ◈

LYONS' CORNER HOUSE

1950s

If 1950s Britain were a colour, it would be grey. Smog was a defining feature of its major cities – the Great Smog of 1952 killed over 10,000 people in London and brought the city to a virtual standstill. Rationing, introduced during World War II, finally came to an end in 1954 – nine years after the war ended – when meat and bacon were taken 'off the ration'. Britain may have won the war, but it had been left virtually bankrupt and it was struggling to recover.

Lyons' Corner Houses offered working-class Londoners an escape from this dull, foggy drudgery. These restaurants were the chain's flagships. The largest of them, in Coventry Street, could cater for up to 2,000 people at a time, making it the largest restaurant in the world. Each of the five floors had a different menu, with a different theme. Art-deco styling and live orchestras made the Corner Houses considerably more stylish than a works canteen, and a little more up-market than the ABC cafés, run by Lyons' rival, the Aerated Bread Company.

At a time when most people's annual holiday was a week at the seaside, this menu of 'Special Continental Delicacies' whisked diners off on a European tour.– on board a slice of toast. Everything was on toast. You may have had the choice of hot or cold, but there was always toast.

Lyons' *Viennoisse*, *Italienne* and *Salade Provençale* introduced many English diners to sophisticated European ingredients such as olives, salami and anchovies for the first

Waitresses at Lyons' Corner House on the first day of opening.

1 **BISMARK 9d.**
Brown Bread and Butter, Pickled Herrings, Potato Salad, Tomato, Lettuce.

2 **NORVÉGIENNE 1/7**
Buttered Toast, Smoked Salmon, Lemon, Caviare.

3 **OXFORD 1/2**
Buttered Toast, Tomato, Egg, Prawns, Potato Salad, Peas.

4 **ITALIENNE 10d.**
Mixed Italian Salamis with French Bread and Butter.

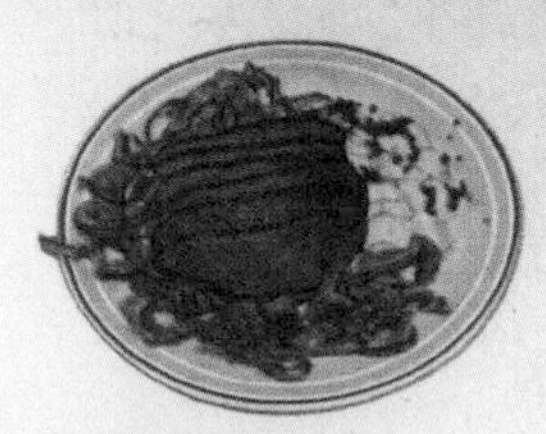

12 **TYROLIENNE 1/6**
Buttered Toast, Sliced Underdone Steak, Potato Salad, Fried Onions.

13 **ANGLAISE 1/2**
Buttered Toast, Roast Beef, Potato Salad, Lettuce, Horseradish & Watercress.

14 **SALADE PROVENÇALE 11d.**
Buttered Toast, Tomato, Potato Salad, Lettuce, Egg, Fillet of Anchovies, Fillet Smoked Herrings.

15 **POJARSKI 10d.**
Buttered Toast, Chicken Cutlet, Potato and Peas Salad, Tomato, Lettuce.

time. They combined these with workaday ingredients like potato salad, ham and lettuce, to create meals that weren't unfamiliar, but were a little bit more interesting than they needed to be. A little bit better than people had come to expect.

The mere fact that these menus were printed in full colour with photos of the food on offer was a revelation. It was a marketing device that Lyons would go on to use in its chain of Wimpy burger restaurants, the first of which opened in Oxford Street in 1954.

In Britain in the 1950s, a French restaurant represented the pinnacle of sophistication. And even if your food wasn't French, you could elevate it a degree or two by describing it in something akin to French. At Lyons, even the most Anglo-Saxon of meals are given names with a French twist – ham and tomatoes on toast is *Yorkaise* and roast beef on toast is *Anglaise*. However, hidden in the language is a tiny reminder that we haven't totally embraced European cuisine – the sliced steak in the *Tyrolienne* is described, not as pink or rare, but as 'underdone'. In other words, not cooked as thoroughly as it should be!

They may not have been the Savoy, but the Corner Houses were a little bit of affordable luxury, and people visited them in their millions. It's hard to find anyone who lived in London or visited the capital in the 1950s who doesn't remember being taken to a Corner House for a birthday treat or a first date. They were as London as red buses, black taxis and bombsites. ◈

Front cover of the Lyons' Corner House menu.

LAST DINNER AT ELBULLI

30 July 2011

SOME MENUS ARE THEMED, SOME MENUS ARE TRADITIONAL AND SOME MENUS are simply a box of delights. During Ferran Adrià's reign as head chef at the Catalan restaurant elBulli, diners were treated to the finest examples of molecular gastronomy, the acceptable face of playing with your food.

The Michelin three-star restaurant on the Costa Brava had been operating successfully for 25 years when Adrià took the helm in 1987. His new approach to cooking ensured that elBulli (named after the owners' bulldogs) soon became known internationally as the kind of place where you were as likely to be given forceps as a fork to eat your food, while fish and chips meant a disc-shaped olive-oil chip and clam meringue.

Tobacco-flavoured 'smoked mousse' foam and unconventional experimental dishes such as Parmesan frozen air might not be everybody's cup of tea, but more than a million people a year tried to book a table there. Of these, only around 8,000, forking out £250 a head (excluding drinks), were lucky enough to be seated. Despite such demand, Adrià insisted that elBulli never made any money, indeed that it lost £400,000 a year because it was closed for long periods as new menus were prepared, and stayed afloat only thanks to endorsements, books and advertising contracts.

The final meal was served at the end of July 2011 in a special 49-course extravaganza which featured favourite dishes from the restaurant's back catalogue. The first item on the menu is a good indication of what was to follow – a dry Martini which came not in a glass but as a small spherical blob of reconstituted olive juice sprayed with gin and vermouth while on your tongue. Among the dishes that followed were:

- SPHERICAL OLIVES – made using Adrià's spherification technique and filled with concentrated olive liquid.

- ☐ 1: Dry martini
- ☐ 2: Mojito-caipirinha
- ☐ 3: Mojito and apple baguette
- ☐ 4: Gin fizz
- ☐ 5: Spherical olives
- ☐ 6: Mimetic peanuts
- ☐ 7: Pistachio ravioli
- ☐ 8: Parmesan cheese porra
- ☐ 9: Parmesan cheese macaron
- ☐ 10: Gorgonzola balloon
- ☐ 11: Olive-oil chip
- ☐ 12: Flower in nectar
- ☐ 13: Flowers paper
- ☐ 14: Tender almonds
- ☐ 15: Pa amb tomàquet
- ☐ 16: Golden egg
- ☐ 17: Clam meringue
- ☐ 18: Liquid croqueta
- ☐ 19: Smoked mousse
- ☐ 20: Squid and coconut ravioli
- ☐ 21: Soy cristal
- ☐ 22: Nori ravioli with lemon
- ☐ 23: Matches
- ☐ 24: Niguiri
- ☐ 25: Boiled shrimp
- ☐ 26: Two cooking prawns
- ☐ 27: Roses with ham wonton and melon water
- ☐ 28: Ham and ginger canapé
- ☐ 29: Cheese bread
- ☐ 30: Icy quinoa of duck foie gras
- ☐ 31: Ajo blanco
- ☐ 32: Veal bone marrow with caviar
- ☐ 33: Pinenuts shabu-shabu
- ☐ 34: Liquid hazelnut porra
- ☐ 35: Curry chicken
- ☐ 36: Lobster ceviche
- ☐ 37: Oaxaca taco
- ☐ 38: Gazpacho and ajo blanco
- ☐ 39: Sea cucumber
- ☐ 40: Hare fritter
- ☐ 41: Game meat cappuccino
- ☐ 41: Blackberry risotto with game and meat sauce
- ☐ 43: Hare loin with its own blood
- ☐ 44: Spice plat
- ☐ 45: 'Bones' of iced tea shavings with sugared mint
- ☐ 46: Raspberry infusion
- ☐ 47: Melba cornet
- ☐ 48: Fondue melba
- ☐ 49: Box

- MOJITO AND APPLE BAGUETTE – instead of boring old bread, the 'baguette' is dehydrated methylcellulose foam featuring clarified apple juice.
- MIMETIC PEANUTS – looks like a peanut, but is in fact thin peanut cream within a crisp skin.
- GORGONZOLA BALLOON – an ostrich-egg-sized sphere of frozen Gorgonzola cheese with nutmeg sprinkled on top. It melts fast, so you need to eat it quickly and in quite large chunks to prevent it disintegrating in your fingers.
- GAME MEAT CAPPUCCINO – game meat soup with a meaty froth topping.
- FLOWERS PAPER – a sheet of candyfloss permeated with a mix of geraniums, roses and pansies.
- BOX – a selection of chocolates including what looks like pink coral (dark chocolate encrusted with sour raspberry powder).

In truth, this was not the last meal served at elBulli. After all the paying guests had gone, Adrià put together another menu for about 50 close friends and family. This included a 40kg meringue in the shape of a bulldog made by famed pastry chef Christian Escribà, but the last dish ever served by the culinary alchemist at elBulli was a classic, no-frills peach melba.

CHAPTER THREE

ROYAL AND POLITICAL

WHAT DO YOU GET FOR £200,000 A HEAD IN IRAN? WHY DID PRESIDENT ROOSEVELT SERVE HOT DOGS TO THE KING OF ENGLAND? HOW DOES A PINEAPPLE LINK THE CORONATION OF GEORGE IV AND ROBERT DUDLEY'S FEAST FOR ELIZABETH I?

MENU FOR HENRY VIII ON FLESH DAYS

1526

IN 1526, AS PART OF AN ONGOING BATTLE WITH HIS OPPONENTS AT COURT, Cardinal Thomas Wolsey issued the Eltham Ordinances, a reform to regulate Henry VIII's daily life and enable himself to continue as the power behind the throne. In addition to key moves such as who had access to Henry's bedchamber, part of these new regulations focused on the royal menu.

But while the Ordinances were at least partially about reducing the size of the royal court's annual expenses, they were more about cementing Wolsey's own position than encouraging Henry to practise more moderate portion control. The menu shown overleaf was an everyday bill of fare, so bears little relationship to the headline banquets of Henry's reign, such as the feasting at the Field of the Cloth of Gold to impress Francis I of France in 1520 – in her book *At the King's Table*, Susanne Groom itemises the extravagant arrangements for this which included 216,000 gallons (almost a million litres) of wine, 78 storks and two peacocks (probably in the form of Peacock Royale, a whole peacock, carefully skinned with feathers still in place, then roasted and the skin and feathers re-attached, usually with the beak gilded).

However, there was a vast array of meat on offer at 'dynner' – at a time we would call a very early lunch – including a first course of swan, red deer, custard and fritters. A second course included a huge variety of birds (such as herons, pheasants, plovers and shovelard, a spoon-billed duck), as well as jelly and ipocras, a spiced wine which was a forerunner of sangria. The early-evening supper was along similar lines, along with dowcetts (sweet tarts, sometimes with added meat, a longstanding favourite and served at the coronation of Henry IV in 1399) plus blancmange, fruit, butter and eggs for the second course. The food was served in the Great Hall at Hampton Court in 'messes', dishes to be shared between up to four people. Nobody would eat everything off the menu, but it would all be cooked and available, a little like an all-you-can-eat buffet.

Two breads were on offer for both meals: manchet, the better quality, was made with flour finely sieved through a cloth, while cheat used inferior flour and was heavier. Of course there were gallons of ale to wash it all down.

On 'fish days' – Wednesdays, Fridays and special occasions such as Lent – the menu switched to seafood, which also included seal. Diners could choose from herring, eel, lamprey, pike, salmon, whiting, haddock, mullet, bass, plaice, gurnard, sea bream, sole, conger, porpoise, carp, trout, crab, lobster, sturgeon, tench and perch.

There's plenty of protein, but it's also high in cholesterol, and there is a notable absence of green veg, although it hints at the royal taste in fruit such as baked pippin apples and oranges. Henry liked marmalade, to which he was introduced by his Spanish first wife, Katherine of Aragon, while Wolsey is generally regarded as the first person to serve strawberries and cream together, at a banquet in 1509.

Henry himself ate in private while the rest of the court ate together, the most powerful courtiers in the Great Watching Chamber at Hampton Court and up to 600 others in the Great Hall in two sittings. Right at the bottom of the pile came the maids, servants, porters and children. They had beef and mutton for dinner, and beef and veal for supper. Food that was untouched went to the poor.

Wolsey's Ordinances also went into detail about the cost of each meal and exactly how much food the varying levels of people at court were allowed to eat, as well as enforcing working practices to ensure that master cooks clothed the scullions, the most menial kitchen servants, who had previously been going about their duties naked.

Sadly for Wolsey, his power play was not a long-term success. By 1530, he had failed to get a marriage annulment for Henry, lost possession of Hampton Court and died on the journey to London where he was to face a charge of treason.

The Wardrobe of ye Bedds ——— j s
The Groome ye Porter ——— j s
The Queenes Mayds sorts ——— iij s

A Declaration of the particular Ordinaunces of Fare for the Dietts to be served to the Kings Highnes, the Queenes Grace, and the Lords, with the Household as hereafter followeth./

The Diett for the Kings Maty and the Queenes Grace of like fare In all two Messes as followeth.

On a flesh day

Dynner

Cheat Bread & Manchet ——— [illegible]
Beare and Ale ——— [illegible]
Wyne ——— [illegible]
Flesh for Pottage ——— [illegible]
Chines of Beef ——— [illegible]
[illegible] ——— [illegible]
Venison in brewis or [illegible] ——— [illegible]
[illegible] of [illegible] or Mutton ——— [illegible]
[illegible] in [illegible] ——— [illegible]
Swanne, or Goose, [illegible] ——— [illegible]
Capons of gr ——— [illegible]
Conyes of gr ——— [illegible]
[illegible] bake [illegible] ——— [illegible]
Custard garnished or [illegible] ——— [illegible]

Supper

Cheat Bread & Manchett ——— [illegible]
Beere & Ale ——— [illegible]
Wyne ——— [illegible]
Flesh for pottage ——— [illegible]
[illegible]
Chickens in [illegible] Larke Sparrows or Lambe stewed [illegible] of Mutton ——— [illegible]
Giggots of Mutton or Venison stopped with Cloves ——— [illegible]
Capons of gr ——— [illegible]
Conyes of gr ——— [illegible]
Phesant, Herne, [illegible] or ——— [illegible]
[illegible], [illegible], or [illegible] ——— [illegible]
[illegible] or Orange ——— [illegible]
Quinces, or [illegible] ——— [illegible]

ROBERT DUDLEY'S FEAST FOR ELIZABETH I

1560

If the way to a woman's heart is through her stomach, then Elizabeth I really should have married Robert Dudley. Between her accession to the throne in 1558 and his death 30 years later, he prepared several lavish entertainments for her, all designed to win the hand of the Virgin Queen. This particular feast was to celebrate the signing of the Treaty of Edinburgh in 1560. In return for his attention, Elizabeth made him Master of the Horse, a Privy Councillor, Lord Steward of the Royal Household and the Earl of Leicester, but she never gave him the main prize.

Serving large water birds such as swan, stork and heron demonstrated status. Fifteenth-century cookery writer Platina even warned commoners against sampling these birds, just in case they developed a taste beyond their station. Even so, these aren't necessarily the most succulent of meats. Wild shoveler ducks can taste nasty because of the insects and weeds they eat, and heron has fallen from our diet altogether. In *Pot-luck; or, The British home cookery book*, written in 1914, May Byron has a recipe for heron pudding, but warns against damaging the bones when preparing it, as the liquid which oozes out tastes unpleasantly fishy.

These birds were served as much for visual effect as for flavour. They would be skinned with their feathers intact. After skinning, they'd be boiled to tenderise them, then roasted. Finally, they'd be redressed with their feathered skin to create a striking if macabre centrepiece. Dudley didn't choose to serve swan or peacock – the most impressive birds at a rich man's table. Perhaps, given the Elizabethans' sophisticated use of visual imagery and symbolism, he was anxious not to suggest that he thought himself the most powerful person in the room.

After the feast came the banquet. This course of sweetmeats, biscuits, sugared fruits and pastes was very popular with Elizabeth, who was noted for her sweet tooth. Sadly, the Elizabethans knew nothing of the connection between sugar and tooth decay – the wealthy even used sugar as a tooth paste – and Elizabeth's fondness for sweet treats would later take its toll. In 1597, the French ambassador, André Hurault, noted that her face was 'long and thin, and her teeth are very yellow and unequal'. The stickiness of these delicacies also made them difficult to eat with just your fingers and a knife, which was still the polite way of eating in company. It was partly to deal with these tricky sweetmeats that the newfangled fork began to make an appearance at the dining table.

MENU

10 sheep

6 herons

48 teal

60 eggs

41 dozen loaves

6 shoveler ducks

26 turkeys

Banquet course

Sweetmeats

Cakes

Exotic fruits, including pineapple

The banquet was another opportunity for Dudley to impress Elizabeth. The centrepiece was an extravagant sculpture in marchpane – a forerunner of marzipan, made with sugar, almonds and rosewater. Marchpane could be moulded into anything from a dragon to a chess set. Elizabeth was particularly delighted by a marchpane model of St Paul's Cathedral, which she was given in 1562. While we don't know the design of Dudley's creation, we do know from the accounts that building it took 86lb (39kg) of sugar. This was at a time when a wealthy family might be expected to consume around 1lb (450g) of sugar a year.

It's worth mentioning that the pineapple that appears in the accounts for the banquet is almost certainly a mistake. When the pages of the accounts were put on display in 2003, *The Times* got very excited to discover this early mention of a pineapple: it was thought not to have arrived in Britain for another 100 years. But in her book *The Pineapple: King of Fruits*, Fran Beauman asserts that, at this time, the word pineapple almost certainly referred to pine nuts, not the fruit. ◈

CORONATION BANQUET OF GEORGE IV

19 July 1821

After the Duke of Wellington's victory at the Battle of Waterloo in June 1815, Britain was arguably the most powerful nation in Europe. George IV was keen that his 1820 coronation should reflect this – outshining Napoleon's imperial coronation of 1804. The result is perhaps the most extravagant, expensive and ridiculous coronation in British history.

The ceremony at Westminster Abbey lasted five hours. George arrived via a raised and canopied walkway, wearing a velvet and ermine robe with an 8m train. He was attended by hundreds of courtiers and servants, all wearing Tudor-inspired costumes. Even the historic St Edward's crown wasn't good enough. He commissioned a new one, encrusted with thousands of pounds' worth of hired jewels, which were later removed and returned after Parliament refused to buy them. The ceremony was followed by an extraordinary banquet at Westminster Hall. This proved so costly that when William IV succeeded his brother in 1830, he decided not to hold a banquet at all. Nor has any monarch since.

The sheer volume of food is extraordinary. It explains why George's waist had expanded to 125cm by the time of his death a decade later. In his 1821 work, *An Authentic History of the Coronation of His Majesty King George the Fourth*, Robert Huish records that 7,442lb (3,375kg) of beef were served, 2,474lb (1,120kg) of mutton and 1,600 chickens were served – to just 300 guests. That's more than 11kg of beef, nearly 4kg of mutton and 5 chickens per person. Each guest could wash down this meat feast with a couple of bottles of champagne, and a similar amount of claret or burgundy.

The crowning glory of the banquet was an 11lb pineapple. The honour of carving this sweet and sticky beast fell to Lord Denbigh and Lord Chichester. The Georgians adored their pineapples – they sculpted them onto their gateposts and they painted them onto their pottery. The cost of growing them domestically or importing them successfully was so high that they were a treat to be enjoyed

80 tureens of turtle soup

40 tureens of rice soup

40 tureens of vermicelli soup

80 turbot

40 trout

40 salmon

80 joints of venison

40 joints of roast beef, including three barons

40 joints of mutton

40 joints of veal

160 dishes of vegetables, including potatoes, peas and cauliflower

240 sauce boats of lobster sauce

120 sauce boats of butter sauce

120 sauce boats of mint sauce

80 dishes of braised ham

80 savoury pies

80 dishes of daubed geese – two in each

80 dishes of savoury cakes

80 pieces of braised beef

80 dishes of braised capons – two in each

320 dishes of mounted pastry

320 dishes of small pastry

400 dishes of jellies and cream

80 dishes of lobster

80 dishes of crayfish

160 dishes of cold roast fowls

80 dishes of cold house lamb

1,200 bottles of champagne

240 bottles of burgundy

2,400 bottles of claret

600 bottles of hock

600 bottles of moselle

60 bottles of madeira

3,500 bottles of sherry and port

100 gallons of ice punch

A pineapple

King George IV's Coronation Banquet, Westminster Hall

only by the very wealthy. It's often reported that less affluent families could hire a pineapple from fruiterers as a centrepiece for a dinner party, returning it untouched the following day, to be hired out again. There's no evidence that this is true, but the success of the myth shows just how rare and treasured they were.

But not everyone in the hall was so well catered for. Wives and families could only watch the banquet from galleries built around Westminster Hall for the occasion. After many hours of witnessing the gourmandising taking place below, the spectators' hunger became unbearable. There are reports of at least one diner wrapping a capon in his handkerchief and hurling it up to his hungry family. Perhaps wives were not invited because George didn't want to draw attention to the absence of his own estranged wife, Caroline of Brunswick. The new king was so fearful that she would try to gatecrash his big day that prizefighters, dressed as footmen, were hired to patrol the perimeter and keep her out.

Any sympathy for these onlookers should be tempered. They were landowners, benefiting from the 1815 Corn Laws which artificially raised the value of their harvests, inflated the cost of bread and led to starvation, protest and riot across the country. As the price of bread rose, wages in the industrial cities fell. Poor pay was pushed down further by the return of thousands of troops from the Napoleonic Wars – the soldiers who had given George his victory over the French and provided him with the spoils of war which paid for his feast. ◈

LUNCH TO CELEBRATE THE ALBERTINE STATUTE

1 March 1848

1848 WAS A YEAR OF REVOLUTION AND REFORM, REACTION AND REPRESSION, right across Europe. In Sardinia, King Carlo Alberto was under increasing pressure to give his people greater religious freedom and more political power in order to avoid these being taken by force. The resulting statute, which established a representative government and equality before the law, was an important step on the road to Italian unification. To celebrate the statute, and to thank those that had delivered it, the Decurion Members of the City of Turin threw a luncheon for 50 guests at the Hotel Europa on 1 March 1848. The statute itself was finally approved by Carlo Alberto three days later.

While it contains an impressive selection of dishes, it's the menu itself that's particularly revealing. To begin with, it's written in Italian. This may seem unremarkable for an Italian menu, but in 1848 any menu worth its salt was written in French. And even Italians didn't speak Italian. When Italy was finally unified in 1861, it's estimated that only about 10 per cent of the population spoke the language. Most spoke a regional dialect or a form of Vulgar Latin. But Italian was the language of the nobility and the civil service across the various kingdoms that had come together to form the new country. Writing this menu in Italian was a political statement. It celebrated the connection between the different states and reinforced the idea of unification.

The illustrations also promote unification. The picture at the top left represents Carlo Alberto's signing of the Lega Doganale in 1847, which created a customs union between Piedmont, Tuscany and the Papal States. This led to a common political strategy, a war of independence and a visit by Carlo Alberto to Genoa later that year. His visit is illustrated at the bottom right-hand side of the menu. The picture of a train at the bottom left represents the planned railway line that would connect Turin, Milan, Bologna, Florence and Rome, and which is still the main line through Italy today. The menu displays an ambition to create a

PRANZO ALLA RUSSA di 50. COPERTI dato dal CORPO DECURIONALE
DELLA CITTÀ DI TORINO
SERVITO DA BER.do TROMBETTA.
per Mercoledì 1.° Marzo 1848.

Zuppa di Testuggine

ANTIPASTO.

Fritto misto.
Pesce Turbot a due salze.
Arrosto di Bue all' Inglese (quello del 1.° premio)
Cappone con tartuffi alla Parigina
Certosa di selvaggina

PUNCH ALLA ROMANA.

Piccoli piselli all' Inglese.
Carciofi alla Lionese.
Faggiano allo spiedo con crescione.
Pasticcio di feggato grasso con gelatina.
Plum-puddings al Rhum.
Crema alla Chantilly.

GELATI.

DESSERT.

modern, unified kingdom, without ever saying it.

The food itself is a million miles from the pasta and risotto that we associate with modern Italian cuisine. It's a blend of French and Piedmont styles of cooking that begins with turtle soup, the seemingly mandatory starter of the nineteenth century (see Mrs Beeton's *Dinner for 18 Persons*, page 163, and Duke of Wellington's Waterloo Banquet, page 125). The certosa di selvaggina – a 'monastery of game' – is particularly impressive, made of woodcock, partridge, pigeon, quail and pheasant, laid on a bed of vegetables and beans. There are also some English dishes in there – roast beef and plum pudding would define the British in a thousand political cartoons across the century.

The punch served between the two main courses is something that appears in lots of Italian menus of the time, and is intended to help restore the diners' digestive rigour before the next onslaught of stuffed meats and rich puddings.

The menu also tells us that the meal will be served alla Russa – Russian style – with the different dishes served as separate courses. This new style of service was replacing service *à la francaise* – which presented all the dishes at the same time. (there's more about this in Mrs Beeton's *Dinner for 18 Persons*, page 163). Bernardo Trombetta, owner of Hotel Europa, announces the new style of service in bold lettering on the top of his menu. This may simply reflect his desire to show how 'on trend' his hotel is. But moving away from service *à la française* may also be a way of gently snubbing Italy's nearest neighbour. This would certainly have played well with Carlo Alberto, who had written a few years earlier, 'the most beautiful day of my life will be the day on which there is war with France and I have the good fortune to serve in the Austrian army.'

Sadly, Carlo Alberto wouldn't live to see the unification of Italy. After defeat in the First Italian War of Independence, he was forced to abdicate in favour of his son, Victor Emmanuel, and died in exile in 1849. ◈

WOMEN'S FREEDOM LEAGUE "VICTORY" DINNER

22 February 1918

IN 1918, THE REPRESENTATION OF THE PEOPLE ACT GAVE WEALTHY WOMEN over the age of 30 the right to vote. The Women's Freedom League (WFL) celebrated the new act with a "Victory" Dinner at the Economy Restaurant in Regent Street. The simple menu, printed in WFL green, sets out a modest four-course dinner, followed by coffee.

It's striking that at the top of the menu the word "Victory" is written in quotation marks. This is a reminder that the victory was not yet complete. The act enfranchised over eight million women in Britain, but many more still couldn't vote. All women under 30, and women who didn't own property or have a degree from a British university, still had no say in local or national politics. This menu is celebrating a move forward, but not a final triumph.

While this menu includes a fish course of turbot, the rest of it, including the main course of lentil cutlets in tomato sauce, is vegetarian. There's a strong link between the women's suffrage movement and vegetarianism. Some suffragettes saw the cooking of meat as one of the chores that tied women to domestic duties, others saw eating it as an example of man's abuse of his physical power. For whatever reason, like other radicals of the time, from G. B. Shaw to M. K. Gandhi, many campaigners for women's suffrage adopted vegetarianism as part of their ideology. Maud Joachim, a Scottish-born suffragette who spent time in Holloway Prison, wrote, 'It is a strange fact that many of the militant suffragettes are mostly recruited from the mild vegetarians.'

The WFL even opened its own vegetarian café, the Minerva, offering 'dainty vegetarian lunches'. The café, which attracted men and women of all radical persuasions, made significant profits, which the WFL used to fund its campaigns. The emergence of cafés and tearooms at the end of the nineteenth century was crucial to the women's suffrage movement. Until then, while women could attend

VOTES FOR WOMEN W. F. L.

"Victory" Dinner,

FEBRUARY 22ND, 1918.

MENU.

Consommé Julienne.
ou
Crême de Volaille.

Turbot à la Mornay.
Pommes Nouvellee.

Lentil Cutlets and Tomato Sauce.
Eggs à l'Italienne.

Tarte de Rhubarbe.
Crême à la Vanilla.

Café.

formal meetings and public talks, there were few places outside the home where they could meet to discuss politics and plan a campaign. The pubs, chophouses and coffee shops which had long been the boilerhouses of male political dissent were off limits to respectable Edwardian women. It was the tearooms and cafés that provided them with the informal space their movement needed. Some, like the Minerva, Molinari's and Alan's Tea Rooms, were important because they openly supported the cause of women's suffrage. Others, like the chain cafés of Lyons and ABC, simply provided a place where lower-middle-class women could meet.

And they would need to keep meeting for some time to come. It would take another ten years of campaigning before the Equal Franchise Act of 1928 would give all women the same voting rights as men.

Charlotte Despard leads members of the Women's Freedom League.

LENTIL AND COURGETTE FRITTERS, ROASTED TOMATOES AND TAHINI DRESSING

SERVES 4

For the Lentil Fritters
3 tablespoons olive oil
½ red onion, finely chopped
1 clove garlic, chopped
2 teaspoons ground cumin
2 teaspoons ground coriander
pinch dried chilli flakes
200g (7oz) red lentils
600ml (20fl oz) water or vegetable stock
1 courgette, grated
75g (2½oz) feta cheese
20g (¾oz) flat leaf parsley, chopped
20g (¾oz) chopped mint
3 tablespoons self-raising flour
2 eggs, separated

For the Tahini dressing
200g (7oz) Greek yoghurt
4 tablespoons tahini
1 clove grated garlic
juice 1 lemon
2 teaspoons honey
salt

To serve
200g (7oz) fresh rocket
75g (2½oz) feta cheese
1 courgette, grated
juice 1 lemon
2–3 tablespoons extra virgin olive oil

Heat 2 tablespoons the oil in a sauté pan and add the chopped onion and garlic. Cook for 3–4 minutes on a low heat. Season with salt and add the cumin, coriander and chilli flakes. Stir again before adding the lentils along with the water of vegetable stock. Simmer for 20 minutes or until all the liquid has been absorbed and the lentils are soft. Add the grated courgettes and cook for a further few minutes.

Remove the lentils from the heat, stir through the chopped parsley and mint and crumble in the feta cheese. Season with black pepper and a little more salt if needed. Tip the contents of the pan into a shallow tray and allow it to completely cool down completely.

Make the tahini dressing by combining all the ingredients together in a small bowl. Season to taste. If it's a little thick, add a splash of water.

When the lentils are completely cool, whisk the egg whites to firm peaks in a large clean bowl. Stir the self-raising flour and egg yolks into the cooked lentil mix and stir well before gently folding in the egg whites.

Heat the remaining oil in a large frying pan. When hot, drop in 5–6 tablespoons of the fritter mixture at once and cook for 2–3 minutes or until golden. Turn them over and do the same on the other side. Repeat this until all the mixture is used up. Place the cooked fritters on absorbent paper while you cook the second or third batch.

Mix the rocket with the crumbled feta, grated courgette. Squeeze over the juice of a lemon and a dash of extra virgin olive oil. Serve the fritters on the salad and drizzle with the tahini dressing. Serve a little more on the side to dip.

HAMPSTEAD COMMUNIST PARTY FIRST ANNUAL DINNER

11 December 1920

On 11 December 1920, members of the newly formed Hampstead branch of the Communist Party of Great Britain sat down to their first Annual Dinner. Unsurprisingly, the toasts didn't include 'The King' and there was no mention of Christmas, which was only a fortnight away. Other than that, it was a very ordinary menu – tomato soup, whiting, lamb cutlets, ice cream and cheese – that would have passed into history unnoticed. But in London in 1920 the security services were deeply concerned about the Bolshevik threat. They closely monitored the evening's proceedings, reporting every detail to Cabinet, including the menu, which has only recently been declassified by MI5.

The food itself is standard fare for the lower middle classes. But other items on the menu are more interesting; 'The Ladies' are toasted as they would have been at the local golf club, but so is 'The International'. And while 'comrades' are initially entertained by pianoforte solos, the evening is concluded with a rendition of the 'Prolotarion [sic] Anthem – The Red Flag'.

Even the quote at the top of the menu, 'The Tocsin of the Soul, The Dinner Bell', may have alarmed the paranoid authorities. It's an uncredited quote from Lord Byron, a radical politician as well as a poet, whose first speech to the House of Lords included a passionate defence of 'the mob':*'it is the mob that labour in your fields and in your houses – that man your navy and recruit your army – that have enabled you to defy all the world and can also defy you when neglect and calamity have driven them to despair.'* Byron's isn't the only name missing from the menu. In *The Secret Twenties: British Intelligence, the Russians and the Jazz Age*, Timothy Phillips suggests that the unnamed guest of honour was Soviet spy Nikolai Klyshko. Klyshko's mission was to help spread Communist ideology. But promoting the fall of Capitalism demands capital. Shortly before the dinner, he'd arrived back in Britain carrying two suitcases. Both were packed with platinum bars.

F I R S T A N N U A L D I N N E R

To to hold at

RESTAURANT PINOLI

Wardour Street, W.

On Saturday, 11th December, 1920.

"The Toscin of the Soul,
The Dinner Bell".

at Seven p.m.

Under the Chairmanship of

COMRADE HARRY HEASE

Menu

Hors d'Ouvre Varies

Tomatoo Soup

Freid Fillit of Whiting

Lamb Cutlets
Vegetables

Chicken au Chassrole

Salade

Ices

Cheese

Café

TOASTS

"The Chairman's Penediction"

"The Communist Party"
Proposed by Mr. F WILLIS
Responded by Mr MacLaine
Pianoforte Solo

"The Ladies"
Proposed by Jim Connel
Responded by A "LADY"
Song
"The International"
Proposed by Mr. PALME DUTT
Responded by Mr. E. Burns
Pianoforte Solo

"The Hampstead Communist Party"
Proposed by Mr. A EDWARDS
Responded by Mr. E.A. TOVEY

Prolotarion Anthem – "The Red Flag

WOMEN'S FREEDOM LEAGUE VICTORY BREAKFAST

Hotel Cecil, 5 July 1928

IN 1918, WEALTHY WOMEN OVER THE AGE OF 30 WON THE RIGHT TO VOTE. THE Women's Freedom League celebrated with a victory dinner (see page 72). In 1928, the Equal Franchise Act gave women the same voting rights as men. This time they celebrated with a breakfast.

A breakfast celebration is unconventional but entirely appropriate for members of the WFL. During the years of campaigning, hundreds of members had been imprisoned for non-violent acts of disobedience. On the morning of a campaigner's release from prison, supporters would meet them at the prison gates and take them for a celebratory breakfast at one of the cafés sympathetic to their cause. Speaking at the 1928 Victory Breakfast, Mr Pethick-Lawrence, husband of the WFL's Chairman (sic), told the 250 guests, 'This recalls the famous breakfasts we used to have in the old fighting days when the prison gates were opened.'

The Victory Breakfast was served at Hotel Cecil on the north bank of the Thames. With over 800 rooms, it was the largest hotel in Europe and had a legendary jazz orchestra in its Palm Court. Some 600 people could dine in its Grand Hall and a further 350 in its Victoria Hall. It was a far cry from the Economy Restaurant in Regent Street which had hosted the 1918 celebration.

There's a simplicity and elegance to the menu – this is the 1920s, after all. Bacon and eggs are just that. There are no mushrooms, tomatoes or hash browns to complicate matters. And there's a choice of fish. The only surprising items on the menu are cucumber and lettuce.

Lots of menus include a toast to 'the ladies' (see page 92), often a patronising thank you for the hard work the 'ladies' have done, preparing a meal they've been excluded from. But here the list of reassuringly entitled 'Short Speeches' includes one from Viscountess Rhondda to 'the Men Who Have Helped Us'. According to the *Guardian*'s report of the breakfast, she reminded people that 'the men deserved

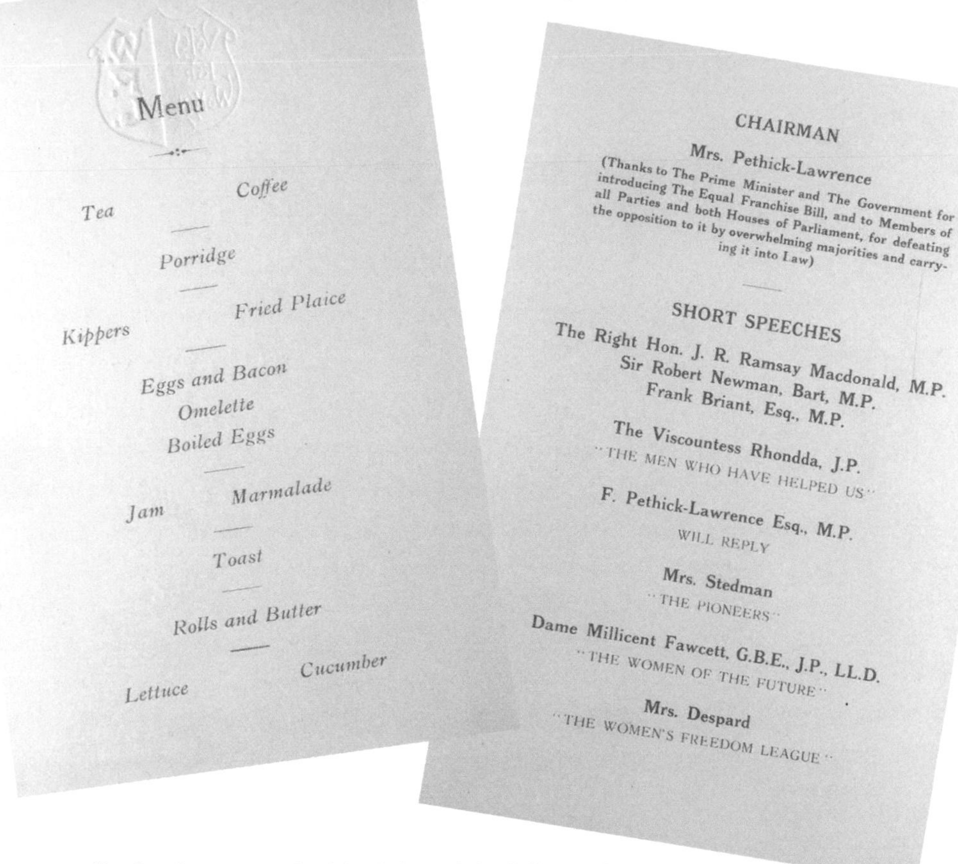

more credit, for the women had had the prick of discomfort to spur them on.'

But hidden among the names of speakers is the remarkable story of a truly progressive couple. Emmeline Pethick was a socialist and a campaigner. Frederick Lawrence was an Eton-educated Liberal barrister. They met and fell in love, marrying in 1901. She didn't take his name and they never shared a bank account. But she converted him to both socialism and the woman's suffrage movement. The couple were arrested and imprisoned following a demonstration in 1912, and after their release were expelled from the Women's Social and Political Union for opposing violent protest. Emmeline went on to become Chairman of the WFL and Frederick was elected Labour MP for Leicester West in 1923. His name, along with that of Emmeline and 57 other women, appears on the statue of suffragette leader Millicent Fawcett, which was unveiled in Parliament Square in London in April 2018. ◈

FRANKLIN ROOSEVELT'S STATE PICNIC WITH KING GEORGE VI

11 June 1939

Official state dinners at the White House have almost always been formal sit-down affairs. King David Kalakaua of Hawaii was the first invitee, hosted by President Ulysses S. Grant in 1874. The King came with his own royal food tasters and enjoyed a 20-course meal.

Sometimes these dinners are merely forums for genteel diplomacy, but President Franklin Roosevelt had a much more serious motive when he invited King George VI in June 1939. George was the first reigning British monarch to visit America, and relations between the two countries had not always been cordial. Roosevelt, though, was keenly aware that Europe was once again close to plunging itself into a major conflict and wanted to align the US and Britain more closely, despite a powerful isolationist lobby keen to make America great again.

Long story short, the President's carefully laid plans went swimmingly. Roosevelt and the King discussed military tactics and the importance of naval collaboration while crowds packed the streets of Washington DC to catch a glimpse of the King and Queen Elizabeth. There were various concerts, a trip on the presidential yacht down the Potomac to Mount Vernon, and at Arlington Cemetery the royal couple laid a wreath at the Tomb of the Unknown Soldier.

Then things became more informal. The Potus and Flotus hosted the monarchs at their private home, Springwood, in Hyde Park, New York, to show that they were all just regular people, hanging out together, going for a swim in their private swimming pool. And instead of a ceremonial banquet, they went for a picnic on the estate at their Top Cottage retreat. Hot dogs were the order of the day (served on a silver tray but eaten off paper plates) and made the headlines, not least because they were a culinary first for the King. 'King tries hot dog and asks for more,' chuckled the *New York Times*. 'And he drinks beer with them.' They were a hit. The King ate his 'with gusto' and asked for seconds, while the Queen

First Lady Eleanor Roosevelt, Franklin D. Roosevelt, Sara Roosevelt, Queen Elizabeth and King George VI, Hyde Park, New York, 1939.

MENU

Virginia ham

Hot dogs

Cold turkey

Sausage

Cranberry jelly

Green salad

Rolls

Strawberry shortcake

Coffee, beer, soft drinks

was unsure how to consume them and went for the knife-and-fork option rather than taking FDR's advice: 'Push it into your mouth and keep pushing it until it is all gone.'

The tour was a success, the American public was captivated and the path to co-operation had been successfully smoothed out.

Roosevelt was not the only President who could play it cool. When West German Chancellor Ludwig Erhard visited Lyndon Johnson a month after JFK had been assassinated in 1963, he was served barbecued spare ribs, pinto beans, coleslaw and apricot pies, with strong coffee and beer. Erhard gave Johnson a bottle of lovely sweet white wine, a fine 1959 Piesporter Goldtröpfchen from the Reichsgraf von Kesselstatt estate. In return, Johnson gave Erhard a Stetson. ◈

INDEPENDENCE NIGHT IN INDIA

Taj Mahal Palace Hotel, Mumbai, 1947/2017

On the eve of their country's independence, 14 August 1947, Indians began celebrating on the streets as British colonial rule finally came to an end. In Bombay (now Mumbai), huge numbers congregated outside the Gateway of India monument, while at the city's Taj Mahal Hotel guests assembled for a special Independence Night dinner. Among them was Sarojini Naidu, poet, freedom fighter and former President of the Indian National Congress, who had been present at various freedom movement meetings previously in the hotel. Entertainment came from Micky Correa, the hotel's resident big-band leader for many years, Goan trumpeter Chic Chocolate and dancer/choreographer Shirin Vajifdar with her pupils the Marwadi Belles.

Seventy years later, after coming across the menu in its archives, the Taj group decided to re-create the occasion at a number of its hotels in India, as well as at the St James' Court, a Taj hotel in London. In a nice touch, the meal cost 1,947 Indian rupees, although serving and ex-service personnel were given a 70 per cent discount.

There was an Indo-French fusion feel to the menu because under British rule the hotel had been run by French chefs who trained up Indian apprentices. The head chef in 1947 was Miguel Arcanjo Mascarenhas – known as Chef Masci – who had started working at the hotel as a kitchen boy. Throughout the menu there was an emphasis on the idea of

Independence Day celebration procession, 1947.

independence, liberation and India in the names of the dishes. We can't be totally certain about the content of any of the dishes, although one of the original diners was consulted for the 2017 re-creation. This gave the modern chefs considerable freedom to interpret the menu card.

MENU

Consommé à l'Indienne
Velouté d'Amandes

Délices à l'Hindustan

Paupiette de Saumon Joinville

Poularde Soufflé Independence
Legumes Varies

Vacherin de Pêches Liberation
Friandises

Café

With a little variation around the country in terms of names and ingredients, both meals started with a Consommé à l'Indienne (clear soup with Indian spices in 1947, chicken in 2017, flavoured with cumin and coriander) or Velouté d'Amandes, a thick almond soup. Lack of documentation means we can't be sure what the original Délices à l'Hindustan were, but in the new menu they became tamarind-flavoured paneer steaks grilled with mint, coriander and tamarind chutney or, in some hotels, kebabs served on a stick of sugar cane.

These were followed by Paupiette de Saumon Joinville (stuffed salmon roulade), or Poularde Soufflé Independence, morphing into chicken omelette in 2017. There were no vegetarian options on the 1947 menu, so in 2017 the hotel added truffle and wild mushroom vol-au-vent in a cheese and paprika sauce, or spinach crepes filled with makhani sauce. Finally, there was Vacherin de Pêches Liberation, poached peaches with apricot sorbet, then chocolate liqueurs, tea and coffee.

There were other Independence Dinners that night around the city, though none as splendid, in line with the food rationing which was in place at the time. ◈

THE SHAH OF IRAN'S CELEBRATION OF 2,500 YEARS OF THE PERSIAN EMPIRE

14 October 1971

IN AN ATMOSPHERE OF GROWING UNREST WITHIN HIS COUNTRY, SHAH Mohammad Reza Pahlavi of Iran flew in 18 tonnes of food from Paris to celebrate 2,500 years of the Persian Empire. Kings, princes and presidents were entertained for three days in a purpose-built city of tents, erected amid the ruins of the ancient city of Persepolis. The Shah hoped that the event would help to secure his dynasty's reputation, showing the world the modern, secular face of an old civilisation. In fact, the arrogance and extravagance of the festivities helped to fuel support for his opposition and pave the way to his downfall.

Entertaining on this scale had not been seen since the Sun King Louis XIV held picnics at Versailles in the seventeenth century. Maxim's in Paris, the most famous restaurant in the world, closed for two weeks so that its chefs and waiters could orchestrate events in Iran. They were supported by armies of Swiss waiters in suits of deepest blue – the colour of the Persian imperial court. Some 15,000 trees were flown in to create a forest, and water was transported across the desert to keep them alive. The forest was filled with 50,000 songbirds, all of which had been flown in from Europe and all of which died within days because of the extreme temperatures. Almost 50km of silk transformed the Parisian-designed accommodation into a fantasy village of Persian tents, complete with fountains and a new golf course. If you weren't there in person, not to worry: filmmakers were flown in from Hollywood to record the event and create a celebratory film that would be narrated by Orson Welles. If it could be plated in gold, it was.

Amongst the 500 guests were Imelda Marcos, First Lady of the Philippines, Marshal Tito of Yugoslavia, King Hussein of Jordan, Emperor Haile Selassie of Ethiopia and the Romanian leader Nicolae Ceausescu. Queen Elizabeth managed to sidestep the vulgarity, sending her husband, the Duke of Edinburgh, and their daughter Princess Anne in her place. In fact, many heads of state sent

MENU

Quails' eggs stuffed with caviar
Champagne de Château de Saran

Crayfish mousse
Château Haut Brion Blanc 1969

Roast saddle of lamb with truffles
Château Lafite Rothschild 1945

Champagne sorbet made from
1911-vintage Moët

Roast peacock stuffed with foie gras and
surrounded by its court of stuffed quails,
with a nut and truffle salad
Musigny Comte de Vogue 1945

Turban of glazed figs with raspberries
Dom Pérignon Rosé 1959
Cuvée Ravissime

Coffee
Cognac Prince Eugène from Maxim's

2500th Anniversary of the Persian Empire celebratory dinner.

their deputies, but all were nervous about offending the Western-friendly leader of this oil-rich nation.

The menu is a perfect demonstration of the Shah's extraordinary wealth and his lack of connection with his people and their culture. The dishes are almost entirely European, not only in their style, but in their ingredients too. Only the figs and caviar came from Iran. Even the lamb, which is a central ingredient in lots of Iranian cooking, was flown in from Paris and cooked in a quintessentially Western style. European chefs prepared the food and European waiters served it.

The item that made headlines around the world was the roast peacock. The peacock is the symbol of the Persian royal family, and 50 birds, surrounded by courtiers of quails stuffed with foie gras, were served up to the guests. The dish was accompanied by Musigny Comte de Vogue 1945. If you'd like a bottle of this today, you'd better have at least £2,000 in your pocket. The serving of wine with every course was a further reminder that this may have been a Muslim country, but it wasn't a Muslim menu. All the wines were of the finest and rarest vintages. Only 306 bottles of Dom Pérignon Rosé 1959 were ever produced. In 2008, two of them were auctioned by Acker Merrall & Condit for $84,700.

But money was no object in this menu, which allows a page for every course: if in doubt, add some more truffles. Even the sorbet was made with 1911-vintage Moët. It's not surprising that the event is estimated to have cost over £100 million in today's money. That's over £200,000 per guest. This indulgence came at a time when the profits from Iran's oil boom had led to inflation and a widening gap between the rich and poor.

Exiled in Paris, Ayatollah Khomeini said, 'Let the world know that these celebrations have nothing to do with the noble, Muslim people of Iran. All those who take part are traitors to Islam and the Iranian people.' Eight years later, after the Shah was overthrown, he would become the first leader of the Islamic Republic of Iran. ◈

CHAPTER FOUR

FEASTS AND CELEBRATIONS

Enjoy a wedding breakfast with Elvis, then a more refined one with Charles and Diana. Spend Christmas with the Cratchits, then enjoy the festive offering at Alcatraz prison. And go back in time to relax at the first Burns Night Supper or take a risk with swan neck pudding…

MENU FOR THE FUNERAL OF NICHOLAS BUBWITH, BISHOP OF BATH AND WELLS

4 December 1424

VERY FEW MEDIEVAL MENUS HAVE SURVIVED OTHER THAN THOSE FOR ROYAL feasts, and indeed this one is among those in a collection held in the British Museum known as 'Two fifteenth-century cookery-books', which also includes Henry IV's coronation feast plans and a dinner for the Festival of the Holy Trinity.

Bubwith (1355–1424) was not only a bishop (London, Salisbury, and Bath and Wells) but also Lord Privy Seal and Lord High Treasurer of England who left money in his will to fund almshouses. The menu for his Saturday funeral comes in two two-course sections: above, a meat version for the laity, and below, a fish-based version for the clergy attending.

Although some fifteenth-century dishes are reasonably easy on twenty-first-century ears (if not stomachs – roast heron anyone?), others need a little decoding, such as the very first item, 'Nomblys de roo'. With the best cuts of meat usually kept aside for the better off, this was a pie made up of animal offal, frequently – as in this case – deer and probably for the less well-to-do. The name mutated to become 'umbles', referenced centuries later by Samuel Pepys in his diary (see Samuel Pepys's 'Stone' Feast, page 205), and now best known to us in the phrase 'eating humble pie'. There is more deer later on in the 'Aloes de Roo', perhaps from the old French *aloyeaulx*, meaning larks, since these were small pieces of stuffed meat that looked a little like a small bird such as an ortolan (see François Mitterrand's Last – Illegal – Dinner, page 214), a forerunner of beef olives today.

Next is blamangere, the sweet pudding common (and unpopular) as 'blancmange' on school menus of the 1970s. Namechecked in the prologue of Chaucer's *Canterbury Tales*, this version included shredded/ground chicken and rosewater. Also available was braun or 'head cheese' (boiled pig's head turned into a jellified terrine) and chines of pork, a cut from the back of the animal.

Further down there is swan neck pudding (the neck is stuffed with giblets and prepared like a blood pudding), lechemete (a general term which could mean anything from pie or pottage to slices of meat) and finally the crustade, a meat pie often baked with fruits and spices.

Onto the second course, after the deer comes mammenye, a sweet, spiced sauce including honey, ginger, cinnamon, pine nuts, currants and wine, otherwise known as bastard gravy and served on meat. Then you have your rabbit, curlew, pheasant, woodcock, partridge, plover, snipes and 'grete byrds' like swan or goose before coming to yrchouns. This would make an excellent technical challenge on *The Great British Bake Off* – it is pig stomach filled with spicy pork, then covered with slivers of almonds to look like a hedgehog or sea urchin. Lastly there's the cold bakemete, another kind of pie, not necessarily a meat one, made with a lid and described as a pastry 'coffin'. The coffin could sometimes be a bit tough and was not always eaten.

So what could the clerical mourners look forward to? There were some similar dishes – the yrchouns probably contained almond paste instead of meat – but essentially a lot more fish, including herring, cod tails (mulwyl), ling, jellied salmon, whiting, pike and plaice. Instead of nomblys, this first course begins with a fishy broth of eels boiled with parsley in a wine, water and ginger sauce to which was added grated bread. An oddity at the end is the crustade ryal, somewhere between a pie and a spiced quiche but featuring the decidedly non-fishy ingredient of bone marrow.

For the second course, there is more seafood (haddock, hake, sole, gurnard, bream, perch, fried minnows, crabs) and a thick cream of almonds. The main attraction here is the leche lumbard. There are many leche lumbards out there, from a version fashioned like peas in a peapod made out of meatloaf, to spiced date cake/bars, a jelly, and evolving into Lombard/lumer pie, which becomes confused with the humble version. Medieval recipe expert James Matterer, who runs the marvellous Gode Cookery at www.godecookery.com, points out that so many recipes have a Lombardy attribution that it could have been a way of fancifying a dish, in the same way that suggesting a food is French aims to add a high-class effect today. ◈

MENU 1: FOR THE LAITY

FIRST COURSE

Nomblys de roo

Blamangere

Braun, cum mustard

Chynes de porke

Capoun Roste de haut grece

Swan roste

Heroun rostyd

Aloes de roo

Puddyng de swan necke

Vn lechemete

Vn bake, videlicet crustade

SECOND COURSE

Ro styuyd

Mammenye

Connyng rostyd

Curlew

Fesaunt rostyd

Wodecokke roste

Pertryche roste

Plouer roste

Snytys roste

Grete byrdes rosted

Larkys rostyd

Vennysoun de ro rostyd

Yrchouns

Vn leche

Payn puffe

Colde bakemete

MENU 2: FOR THE CLERGY

FIRST COURSE

Elys in sorry

Blamanger

Bakoun heryng

Mulwyl taylys

Lenge taylys

Jollys of samoun

Merlyng sope

Pyke

Grete plays

Leche barry

Crustade ryal

SECOND COURSE

Mammenye

Crem of almaundys

Codelyng

Haddok

Freysse hake

Solys y-sope

Gurnyd broylid with a syryppe

Brem de mere

Roche

Perche

Menus fryid

Yrchouns

Elys y-rostyd

Leche lumbard

Grete crabbys

A cold bakemete

Vn leche

Payn puffe

Colde bakemete

THE FIRST BURNS NIGHT SUPPER

21 July 1801

Few Scots can boast the international fame of poet Robert Burns. It's claimed that, after Queen Victoria and Christopher Columbus, there are more public statues of him than of any other non-religious figure. There are seven in Australia alone. His fame is due, in no small part, to the popularity and proliferation of the Burns Night Supper. From Motherwell to Montreal, Tanzania to Texas, every 25 January, hundreds of thousands of people gather to praise the Bard, pipe in the haggis, drink the whisky and toast the lassies. For one night only, Scotland is the most famous country on the planet.

The simple menu, served with poems and songs, promote not just Burns, but Scotland itself. Perhaps because it celebrates a culture, rather than a religious, political or military victory, Burns Night has been embraced around the world by people who've never heard of the Cheviot Hills. It's even celebrated by the Auld Enemy south of the border – the first Burns Supper in Oxford was held in 1806.

At the centre of everything is the haggis. It was served at the first supper on 21 July 1801, the fifth anniversary of the poet's death. Hamilton Paul, a local minister, invited eight of Burns' friends to meet at the poet's former cottage in Alloway, Ayrshire. They read Burns' poems, ate the haggis and toasted his

genius. Today, that toast would be made with whisky, which has become almost as synonymous with Burns Suppers as the haggis itself. But, according to historian Rab Houston, in 1801 the toast is more likely to have been made with ale or wine.

The first supper was such a success that the friends decided to meet again the following year, this time on the anniversary of the poet's birth. Within a year, other groups were holding their own suppers, and a year later clubs were formed to promote and formalise the celebrations. Even Sir Walter Scott, who as an ardent Tory and supporter of the Union between Scotland and England was at the other end of the political spectrum from Burns, held a Burns Supper in 1815. Unlike many early nineteenth-century clubs, Burns clubs were as likely to be attended by working-class men as they were by the their middle-classes bosses.

The menu for a Burns Supper hasn't really changed, although many will be glad to see that sheep's head has fallen from favour. Nor have the ingredients for a haggis altered: sheep's heart, liver and lungs, oats, fat, onions, herbs and spices, boiled in a sheep's stomach. Although, according to the *QI* website, 33 per cent of Americans think the haggis is a wild beast, hunted on the Scottish moors.

The origins of haggis go back to Greek and Roman times. Food historian Catherine Brown even asserts (to the annoyance of many Scots) that the first reference to haggis as we know it comes from England. Gervase Markham's *The English Hus-Wife,* published in 1615, refers to the dish more than a hundred years before it's in any Scottish texts. But by the time Tobias Smollett wrote the novel *Humphrey Clinker* in 1771, haggis belonged to Scotland – 'I am not yet Scotchman enough to relish their singed sheep's head and haggis,' Clinker complains.

Most feasts have grand and extravagant dishes at their centre – venison, a peacock or at least a turkey. It seems fitting that Burns, a political radical who believed in the equality of man, should be celebrated with a peasant dish that, while not to everyone's taste, is well within the reach of most people's pockets.

THE CRATCHITS' CHRISTMAS MENU

25 December 1843

The Cratchits' Christmas celebrations are the sugary heart of Dickens' *A Christmas Carol*. First published on 19 December 1843, the novel was an instant hit, selling out before Christmas Eve. Over the last 175 years its popularity has never waned. For many, there is no Christmas without the ghostly redemption of Ebenezer Scrooge.

It's often said that Dickens invented Christmas. This is a bit of an exaggeration, but the 1840s was certainly a big decade for the festival and Dickens played his part. In 1843, just as *A Christmas Carol* was being printed, so was the first Christmas card – a picture of a family sitting down to a festive dinner. In 1848, an engraving of the Royal family decorating their tree started a middle-class mania for the Christmas pine. The 1840s also saw the invention of the Christmas cracker – jokes from which are still in use today. The mood of Christmas was changing, and Dickens was helping it along.

Since the Middle Ages, Christmas had been about over-indulgence. Landowners entertained their workers, friends and family with several days of feasting and revelry. It's the spirit of merriment and misrule that led the Puritans to ban Christmas during the Commonwealth (1649–60). But by the middle of the nineteenth century, the industrial revolution meant the old style of celebration was almost impossible. Unlike the farms, factories ran twelve months of the year, so the dark days of winter no longer offered a temporary respite for workers. Christmas needed reinventing for an industrial age. The Cratchits, with help from Queen Victoria and Prince Albert, did just that.

The Cratchits' menu is a modest one. It's only when the goose is 'eked out by apple-sauce and mashed potatoes' that there's enough to go around. But their joy is not diminished by this. On the contrary: the goose's 'tenderness and flavour, size and cheapness, were the themes of universal admiration'. Similarly, the pudding is small and doused in just 'half of half-a-quartern of brandy' – about

Bob Cratchit's Christmas Dinner.

1fl oz! The Cratchits' pleasure doesn't come from medieval-style indulgence, but from making the most of the little they have. It doesn't come from a large gathering, but from having every member of their family around the fire – if only for one evening. This meagre menu and cheerful attitude helped Dickens put family and sentimentality at the heart of the Victorian Christmas.

In the spirit of Tiny Tim, we should spare a thought for the poor Victorian goose. If geese want to travel long distances, they rely on their wings rather than their feet. But if you're a farmer in 1843 and want to bring your geese to a Christmas market, feet are your only option. Large gaggles of geese were driven like cattle from Norfolk to London. They even had little leather boots made to protect their tender feet on the long journey.

MENU

Goose

Gravy

Sage and onion stuffing

Mashed potatoes

Apple sauce

Christmas pudding blazing in half of half-a-quartern of ignited brandy

Apples

Oranges

Roast chestnuts

Hot gin and lemons

CHRISTMAS DAY IN ALCATRAZ PRISON

1929

When prisoners arrived at the famous Alcatraz Federal Penitentiary just off the coast of San Francisco, they were informed: 'You are entitled to food, clothing, shelter and medical attention. Anything else that you get is a privilege.' However, the first inmates were lucky that their warden, James A. Johnston, believed that good food encouraged good behaviour. Consequently, Alcatraz's menus – such as the one opposite for Christmas Day – were regarded as the best in the entire prison service: at other times of the year they offered items such as jambalaya, raspberry buns and purée mongole, a creamed split-pea-and-tomato soup.

Breakfast was at 6.55 a.m., lunch at 11.20 a.m., and dinner at 4.25 p.m.. Each meal was prepared and served by the prisoners under fairly close supervision (they were frisked constantly to make sure they didn't pinch anything sharp) and was extremely filling, averaging around 3,000 calories per day compared to the 2,000 of most other federal prisons. Everybody at the prison – inmates, guards and staff – ate together. Alcatraz was initially used as a military prison before becoming a high-security home to some of the country's most notorious and troublesome inmates, including Al Capone and Robert Stroud, known as the Birdman of Alcatraz. But there were only around 260 prisoners at any one time, so food did not have to be prepared in vast quantities and consequently quality did not suffer.

Inmates were given a tray with five sections to keep the various foodstuffs away from each other before moving to the communal tables. They then had 20 minutes for their meals and were allowed to eat as much as they wanted as long as they didn't leave anything on their plates – those who did lost privileges. Nor were they allowed to talk. At the end of the meal, all cutlery (including, surprisingly, rather sharp steak knives) was laid out and counted to make sure nobody had removed it for nefarious purposes. If things did go wrong, the dining

MENU

Cream celery soup *Saltine crackers*

Roast young turkey *Vegetable dressing*

Cranberry sauce *Giblet gravy*

Combination salad

Mayonnaise dressing

Creamed mashed potatoes *Candied sweet potatoes*

Asparagus tips on toast

White celery *Mixed sweet pickles*

Chocolate layer cake *Walnut layer cake*

Fruit cake *Mince pie*

Bananas *Apples*

Parker House rolls

Coffee *Milk* *Butter*

Mixed candies

Cigarettes

hall had tear-gas canisters on the ceiling which could be triggered if necessary. Thus it earned its nickname, 'the gas chamber'.

The food was still good 25 years later, though still hardly exotic. Here's the menu for Christmas 1954, on which day Catholic mass was held at 8.30 a.m. and at 1.30 p.m. there was a showing of *Secret of the Incas* starring Charlton Heston:

Stuffed celery
Ripe olives
Roast tom turkey
Oyster dressing
Giblet gravy
Snowflake potatoes
Buttered peas
Cranberry sauce
Parker House rolls
Bread and oleo
Pumpkin pie
Fruitcake
Coffee

Most of the dishes are self-explanatory but a few may be unfamiliar. Snowflake potatoes are white potatoes mashed with sour cream and cream cheese, oleo is margarine and a Parker House roll is a sweet bread roll made by flattening a dough ball into an oval and then folding it in half.

Alcatraz Penitentiary closed on 21 March 1963, and here is the final breakfast menu for that day:

Assorted dry cereals
Steamed whole wheat
Scrambled egg
Fresh milk
Stewed fruit
Toast
Bread
Butter
Coffee

ELVIS AND PRISCILLA PRESLEY'S WEDDING BREAKFAST

1 May 1967

The King of Rock 'n' Roll married Priscilla Beaulieu at the Aladdin Hotel in Las Vegas on 1 May 1967. The ceremony lasted just eight minutes and only 14 people witnessed the couple promise to love and honour one another – Elvis is said to have asked to remove the word 'obey'.

By showbiz standards, the reception was a fairly modest affair. There were just a hundred guests for a buffet lunch, and the only celebrity invited was comedian Redd Foxx. The couple's first dance, like so many since, was to 'Love me Tender'.

Although the couple were clearly in love – they'd been living together in Graceland for over five years – some people believe that their wedding was a PR event staged by Elvis's manager, 'Colonel Tom' Parker. By 1967, the Beatles, the Rolling Stones and the Beach Boys had taken over the airwaves. Elvis had topped the charts only once in the previous four years, and Parker was keen to reinvigorate his career. Parker certainly controlled the whole wedding – choosing the venue, restricting the guests and corralling the press. He may also be responsible for making sure that one of the most famous pictures from the wedding, which hit front pages around

Elvis and Pricilla cutting the wedding cake.

MENU

Ham and eggs

Southern fried chicken

Oysters Rockefeller

Roast suckling pig

Poached and candied salmon

Lobster

Eggs Minnette

Six-tiered wedding cake

Champagne

the world the following day, is of the couple standing next to a wedding cake that could have catered for a showbiz wedding ten times the size. Filled with apricot marmalade and kirsch-flavoured cream, covered with fondant icing and decorated with marzipan roses, it's said to have cost around $3,200 dollars. In 1967, that would have bought a new Chevrolet.

The rest of the menu is Vegas glamour mixed with Southern comfort: oysters and lobsters snuggle up to ham and fried chicken. But even the oysters – a pretty healthy source of protein when eaten raw with a dash of lemon juice or tabasco – are cooked to a recipe from the Deep South that bakes them in butter until their cholesterol levels can hold their own against the fried chicken. It's a recipe so rich that Antoine's restaurant in New Orleans, which invented the dish in 1899, named it after John D. Rockefeller, the man at the top of America's rich list.

According to Marty Lacker, a friend of Elvis since their schooldays and one of his two best men on the day, the only food on the menu that the King really cared for was the ham, eggs and chicken. His fondness for high-fat, high-salt, high-sugar food may be attributable to the poverty of his early life in Tupelo, Mississippi, but it would eventually be a factor in his early death, too. In 1996 Mary Jenkins Langston, who cooked for Elvis for the 14 years up to his death, said, 'The only thing in life he got any enjoyment out of was eating. And he liked his food real rich.' Over the years, she perfected her recipe for Elvis's favourite snack, a fried-banana and peanut-butter sandwich. Apparently, the secret is to toast the bread first so it can hold even more butter, which helps with the frying.

Elvis's last performance was at Market Square Arena in Indianapolis, on 26 June 1977. He died on 16 August that year from a massive heart attack. ◈

BUTTERMILK OVEN 'FRIED' CHICKEN WITH APPLE SLAW

SERVES 4

For the marinade

8 chicken drumsticks
½ teaspoon each salt, sweet paprika and dried oregano
¼ teaspoon garlic powder
200ml (7 fl oz) buttermilk
juice ½ lemon
4 twists black pepper
1 tablespoon vegetable oil

For the coating

100g (3½oz) Panko bread crumbs
50g (1¾oz) cornflakes, crushed
2 tablespoons grated parmesan
1 teaspoon salt
1 teaspoon dried oregano
2 teaspoon sweet paprika
½ teaspoon garlic powder
¼ teaspoon chilli powder

For the Slaw

¼ white cabbage, finely shredded
2 Granny Smith apples, cored and thinly sliced
1 stick celery, finely sliced
½ red onion, peeled and finely sliced
1 carrot, peeled and grated
juice 1 lemon
2 tablespoons buttermilk
1 tablespoon mayonnaise
10g (½oz) fresh mint, shredded
large pinch of salt

Score each chicken drumstick 3 or 4 times to allow the marinade to penetrate and tenderise the meat. Combine all the ingredients for the marinade in a large bowl. Mix well and add the chicken, making sure it is fully coated and covered. Cover the bowl with clingfilm and leave in the fridge for a minimum of 6–8 hours or overnight.

Mix the ingredients for the coating in a shallow tray. Make sure the cornflakes still have some texture to them.

Preheat the oven to 200°C/180°C fan/390°F/gas mark 4. Place a metal rack onto a baking tray and brush or spray with a little vegetable oil.

Remove the chicken from the marinade and lay into the coating. Make sure all areas of the drumstick are generously covered in the coating and place onto the greased rack.

When all the chicken is covered, place the tray into the oven for 40–45 minutes until the drumsticks are golden brown all over and thoroughly cooked in the middle.

While the chicken is cooking, make the apple slaw. Combine all the prepared ingredient in a large salad bowl. Mix well and check for seasoning.

Remove the chicken from the oven and serve while hot with the crunchy slaw.

CHARLES AND DIANA'S WEDDING BREAKFAST

29 July 1981

If you stand close to it, a royal wedding is about a prince and princesses exchanging vows. If you step back a little, it's packed with coded messages about a nation and its relationship with its royal family. This one combined a move towards informality with a respect for tradition – the Band of the Welsh Guards played Haydn's 'Oxen Minuet', shortly after the theme from *Love Story.*

This menu is similar in some ways to that enjoyed by Prince Charles's mother in 1947 and his grandfather in 1923. All include courses named after the royal couple and their families. In 1981, guests enjoyed *Suprême de Volaille Princesse de Galles.* In 1923 they were served *Suprême de Saumon Reine Mary* and *Côtelettes*

Music Programme

1. Selection	BLESS THE BRIDE	*Ellis*
2. Waltz	WESTMINSTER WALTZ	*Farnon*
3. Selection	OKLAHOMA	*Rodgers*
4. Interlude	MOON RIVER	*Mancini*
5. Serenade	NEAPOLITAN SERENADE	*Winkler*
6. March	KING COTTON	*Sousa*
7. Waltz	GOLD AND SILVER	*Lehar*
8. Selection	MY FAIR LADY	*Loewe*
9. Theme	THE PRINCESS OF WALES	*Davies/Jones*
10. Film Theme	LOVE STORY	*Lai*
11. Polka	TRITSCH TRATCH POLKA	*Stauss*
12. Selection	SOUTH PACIFIC	*Rodgers*
13. Minuet	OXEN MINUET	*Haydn*
14. Waltz	BELLE OF THE BALL	*Anderson*

Major D. N. Taylor,
Director of Music, Welsh Guards.

Menu

Quenelles de Barbus Cardinal

....

Suprème de Volaille Princesse de Galles
Fèves au Beuree
Mais à la Crème
Pommes Nouvelles

....

Salade

....

Fraises
Crème Caillée

Les Vins

Brauneberger Juffer Spätlese 1976
Château Latour 1959
Krug 1969
Taylor 1955

d'Agneau Prince Albert. And in 1947, the fish course was *Filet de Sole Mountbatten* and the dessert *Bombe Glaceé Princesse Elizabeth*. Following a tradition like this helps to create continuity. It's also a light-hearted way of celebrating the joining of two families and a consort's new royal status. But it's not subtle. And you have to wonder whether Queen Mary really wanted to have a fish dish named after her.

In 1981, four courses wouldn't have looked out of place at a middle-class wedding at a golf club. Even with unemployment running at 2.5 million, it would have been hard to criticise the couple for over-indulgence. By contrast, Prince Charles's grandfather Albert (later King George VI) had enjoyed a wedding breakfast of nine courses – well beyond the means or experience of his average subject in 1923. Prince Charles's menu told people that his family was a bit like theirs. His grandfather's had told them that his family was very different.

It may seem odd that the menu for a British royal wedding should be written in French. But since the nineteenth century, French had been the language of food and formality. And in 1981 the British still weren't that confident about their nation's food. We'd always feared that the French were better at cooking it and we knew that they were better at describing it. Even strawberries and clotted cream – about as English as a dish gets – is described as *Fraises* and *Crème Caillée*. This would change by the time Charles and Diana's son William married Kate Middleton, 30 years later. The menu was written in English, and proudly boasted the British origins of the food:

Saddle of North Highland Mey select organic lamb
Highgrove spring vegetables
English asparagus
Jersey Royal potatoes, sauce Windsor

By the time Charles and Diana's second son, Harry, got married in 2017, they were serving their guests 'bowl food' – a cross between a canapé and a main meal – including pea and mint risotto, chicken fricassée and slow-roasted pork belly with apple compôte and crackling, eaten standing up. The relationship that each royal generation want to establish with their subjects is written in their wedding menu. ◈

CHAPTER FIVE

SPORTS AND ENTERTAINMENT

Recreate Babette's Feast. Taste gold dust at the Oscars. Try kippers with The Greatest. Pile on the calories with the 1966 World Cup winners. Cook five million meals at the Olympics. Eat cereal at Pixar. Stuff yourself with Spam.

THE FIRST ACADEMY AWARDS CEREMONY DINNER

1929

FROM HALF-BROILED CHICKEN ON TOAST AND LONG BRANCH POTATOES (CHUNKY chips) to 13.5kg of edible gold dust, the food on offer at the official Oscars feast has changed rather dramatically over the years. The first Academy Awards ceremony, on 16 May 1929, was more of an enormous dinner party: 270 guests (each of whom paid $5 to attend) sat down at the Hollywood Roosevelt Hotel in Los Angeles to enjoy a feast of celery, lettuce and tomatoes with French dressing, and consommé Celestine, a clear chicken stock garnished with ribbons of crêpe.

The awards were not broadcast on the radio until the following year, but the thrill of discovering who had won was slightly dented by the announcement of the winners three months before. During the event, Douglas Fairbanks, the then Academy President, handed out all 15 statuettes at a rate of one per minute. The first design for these had been, so the story goes, sketched out on a paper napkin by MGM art director Cedric Gibbons at the Academy's launch party in 1927.

Over the years, various venues have hosted the Oscars event, including the Cocoanut Grove nightclub at the Ambassador Hotel, but after 1942 the banquet element was dropped from the actual ceremony and became more of an after-party event.

MENU

Hors d'oeuvre varie
Celery olives nuts rolls

Consommé Celestine
Filet of sole saute au beurre
Half-broiled chicken on toast
New string beans
Long branch potatoes
Lettuce and tomatoes with French dressing

Vanilla and chocolate ice cream
Cakes

Demi-tasse

(left to right) Gene Raymond, Leslie Howard, Dolores Del Rio and Cedric Gibbons at the Academy Awards Ceremony Dinner,1943.

This has not stopped the occasion, now known as the Governor's Ball, becoming increasingly luxurious, with the formal sit-down dinner format changing in 2012 to waiters circulating with small plates. For the last couple of decades, celebrated chef Wolfgang Puck has led a catering team that now amounts to 250 people serving 1,500 guests. Attendees can look forward to delights such as caviar parfait dusted with 24-carat gold, caramel passionfruit lollipops in the shape of tichy Oscar statuettes, and a hand-carved ice station for sushi and other raw bar delicacies. In 2018, the pastry team put together 7,000 Oscar-shaped chocolates coated in edible gold dust. There are, of course, meat-free, dairy-free, gluten-free and nut-free options and, if that's not enough, a team of around a dozen chefs is on hand to put together special requests.

Puck's shopping list is understandably daunting, including 1,400 bottles of Piper Heidsieck Cuvée Brut, 6,000 cocktail forks and 1,000 hibiscus flowers. But not everything is quite so fancy – mini pizzas and burgers are on hand, as well as dishes such as Key Lime Meringue Cheesecake Taco, Baked Potato with Caviar (one of Brad Pitt's favourites) and Chicken Pot Pie with Truffle (Barbra Streisand's special request). Unused food is donated to the charity Chefs to End Hunger.

MUHAMMAD ALI'S TOP OF THE TOWER BREAKFAST

24 July 1966

On 25 February 1964, the young boxer then known as Cassius Clay beat Sonny Liston to become the Heavyweight Champion of the World and promptly changed his name to Muhammad Ali. In May 1966 he retained his title by beating British heavyweight Henry Cooper. Two months later, he was meeting invited guests for breakfast at London's Top of the Tower – the revolving restaurant on the 34th floor of the General Post Office Tower.

The tower had been officially opened by Prime Minister Harold Wilson the previous year. It was a symbol of the 'white heat of technology' with which Wilson hoped to rebuild Britain. But while the setting was high-in-the-sky, the menu is very down-to-earth. It goes into banal detail about the range of cereals available, as if offering both Shredded Wheat and cornflakes is likely to draw the crowds. Diners who aren't sure if they want to meet Ali may perhaps be swayed by the fact that there will be 'various jams' on offer. The menu makes a vague genuflection to European-style breakfasting by offering fresh fruit salad. But it's served with cream, as if it's a dessert. These odd and uninspiring details may be explained by the fact that the restaurant was run by the holiday-camp legend Billy Butlin.

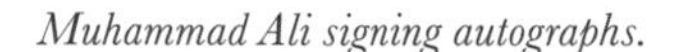

Muhammad Ali signing autographs.

MENU

Fresh juices
orange, tomato, grapefruit

Porridge

Cornflakes

Grapefruit

Shredded Wheat

Eggs, bacon, sausage, tomato

Kidneys and bacon

Poached haddock

Egg and bacon

Kippers

Fresh fruit salad and cream

Tea or coffee

Rolls and butter

Various jams and marmalade

The unlikely combination of venue and menu is perhaps a perfect metaphor for the challenges Wilson's dream would encounter in the coming years, as technological ambition clashed with industrial tradition.

The writer Somerset Maugham suggested that, 'To eat well in England you should have breakfast three times a day.' So perhaps the man regarded by many as the greatest athlete of the twentieth century enjoyed this early-morning feast. He was certainly fond of a large and protein-packed breakfast. The morning after the fight known as 'Rumble in the Jungle', in which he beat George Foreman to regain his world title in 1974, Ali celebrated with a breakfast of two steaks and a dozen scrambled eggs. But it's hard to imagine Usain Bolt or Ronaldo meeting their fans over a bowl of Shredded Wheat and a plate of kidneys. Both dining and celebrity have moved on a long way since 1966.

The traditional English breakfast hit its upper-class zenith in late-Victorian house parties, where trays of kidneys, kippers and kedgeree would be kept warm on sideboards while house guests recovered from their over-indulgence of the night before. Breakfast was a leisurely affair, and the only meal in which reading at table – *The Times*, as likely as not – was socially acceptable. The working classes may not have had the time to prepare kedgeree – the smoked fish, eggs, spice and rice dish that was a staple of the British Raj – but bacon and eggs were fast, fat-filled, salty and satisfying. By the 1950s, it's estimated that half the population of the UK went to work on bacon and eggs – either cooked up at home or served in a 'greasy spoon' café.

Bacon served with eggs is a dish that probably has its origins in Collop Monday, the day before Shrove Tuesday, which in turn was the last day before the fasting of Lent began. Meat would be off the table for Lent, so people would salt any pork they had, turning it into bacon that would keep fresh until they were allowed to eat it again after Easter. Any odds and ends would then be cooked up and eaten with leftover eggs – another no-no for Lent. And so, the great British fry-up was invented one day before the pancake.

Ali's menu stands at a three-way breakfast crossroads. By the end of the 1950s, cereals were increasingly replacing eggs and bacon on Britain's breakfast tables. It led the Egg Marketing Board to fight back with its 'Go to work on an egg' campaign, which ran right through the 1960s and early '70s. At the same time, Victorian breakfast dishes like kedgeree and devilled kidneys were falling out of favour. Here, in 1966, all three traditions meet – the Shredded Wheat, the bacon and eggs and the smoked fish sit on the same menu. By the 1980s, hardly a hotel in London would still be offering guests a kipper.

In October 1980, Ali made his last challenge for the heavyweight title – a failed comeback against Larry Holmes. In the same year, Billy Butlin's restaurant at the Top of the Tower closed its doors for the last time. ◈

ENGLAND'S WORLD CUP BANQUET

30 July 1966

GEOFF HURST SCORED A HAT TRICK (MAYBE), THE CROWD INVADED THE pitch and England beat West Germany 4–2 to become the football champions of the world. Then they went for dinner.

Their menu begins, as you might expect, with a course that any professional sportsman would be happy to take on board – a melon frappé. At its simplest, this is just melon, mint and perhaps a little lemon juice, whizzed up into a healthy and refreshing drink. So far, so good. But then things start to go downhill.

MENU

Melon Frappé

Filets de Sole Véronique

Entrecote Sauté Marchand de Vins
Haricots Verts au Beurre
Pommes Croquettes

Soufflé en Surprise Milady
Bombe Glacée World Cup
Mignardises

Café

WINES

Chablis Chatain, 1er Cru, 1963
Gevrey Chambertin, 1961
Champagne Henkel Trocken
Cognac – Liqueurs

The fish course is *Sole Véronique* – a dish invented in 1898, by legendary chef Georges Auguste Escoffier, to celebrate the première of André Messager's operetta, *Véronique*. The main ingredient is white fish – the protein source of choice for the athletically minded. But this fish is cooked in vermouth, cream and grapes, to create a sauce that's then thickened with butter and flour. This calorie-infested dish is a far cry from the sashimi and quinoa porridge that James Collins, England's head nutritionist during the 2014 World Cup, served up to his players. But to be fair, Collins's team never made it out of the group stage.

By the main course, all caution has been thrown to the wind. Steak cooked in garlic and red wine is served with potatoes that have been mixed with butter and deep-fried in oil. The vegetable is green beans, but these healthy legumes don't hit the table until they've been dressed in a little butter. All this is before the players have cracked the shell of the ice-cream bombe or sampled the tiny French pastries that follow that – just in case they haven't got the fat-to-sugar balance quite right.

The menu may seem a little old-school, but so was the attitude. When the players turned up at the Royal Garden Hotel in Kensington, they discovered their invitation didn't include a 'plus one'. Their wives and girlfriends had to celebrate separately, in another room in the hotel.

The menu also listed the toasts that will be given – Her Majesty the Queen, presidents and heads of states and the Football Association – all to institutions, no mention of players or the game itself. But it doesn't say what time the banquet ends. Perhaps players just leave when they think it's all over.

Wives of the players eating dinner.

MONTY PYTHON'S SPAM CAFÉ MENU

1970

THE MONTY PYTHON TEAM UNLEASHED THEIR FLYING CIRCUS ON BRITISH television viewers in 1969. Four series and four feature films later, the SPAM® sketch remains a firm fan's favourite. At the start, it appears to be just another comedy sketch set in a cliché greasy spoon: grey, humdrum characters are choosing bland English food from a joyless menu. But this is Python; the background characters are all Vikings, the two customers fly in on wires, and all the female caricatures are played by men. Very soon, people will burst into song.

SPAM® is the perfect item for this comedy menu. When American GIs brought it into Britain during the 1940s, it was a miracle – a salty, fatty, satisfying meat you could eat straight from the tin. But by the '70s, it had lost its wartime glamour. It was just a cheap protein source, served up in fritters to unsuspecting schoolchildren or next to limp lettuce and tomatoes to frugal suburbanites. It was the epitome of British lacklustre.

But as the Pythons knew, SPAM® is a great word. Like black pudding, another meat substitute the Python team served up for their viewers, it's a funny word to say. But nobody's quite sure what it means. Even Hormel Foods, the proud creators of SPAM®, who've built a museum to celebrate its glory, refuse to divulge its meaning. Some people think it's short for 'spiced ham' and others 'shoulder pork and ham'. Hormel come down on neither side. Some even think it's short for the slightly less appetising 'special processed American meat'.

While SPAM® may have fallen out of favour in the UK, Hormel's website is proud to tell us that the world consumes 12.8 cans every second. This is despite its not being sold anywhere in Africa or Europe, other than the UK. There are even parts of the world where it's been adopted by the local culture. In Hawaii, where many GIs were stationed during the war, dishes including SPAM® fried with

rice and SPAM® fried wontons, help to make sure that the average Hawaiian consumes 16 cans of the stuff every year. They can even order it in McDonald's.

The menu may be legendary among Python fans, but its legacy reaches around the globe to people who have no idea that there is a Ministry for Silly Walks or that Brian is a very naughty boy. When computer scientists were looking for a word to describe the vast quantities of unwanted and unsolicited mail that clog up our inboxes, they immediately reached for the menu from their favourite greasy spoon, and called it spam. And now for something completely different.

BABETTE'S FEAST

1987

Anyone who has spent hours preparing Christmas dinner, only to watch their loved ones descend into violent disagreements, tantrums and divorce over the sprouts and bread sauce, will be heartened by the restorative and conciliatory effect that Babette's feast has on her diners. Served up in 1987, *Babette's Feast* won the Oscar for Best Foreign Language film. It inspired thousands of professional and amateur chefs to reproduce her extraordinary menu and many more to waste endless hours discussing whether she should have served a different wine with her quail. It's a debate that still simmers along online today.

The film is set in a remote village on the coast of Denmark in 1871. It centres around one extraordinary meal that the exiled Parisian, Babette, cooks for the austere Lutheran community that has taken her in. Their damp, joyless diet of smoked fish and bread porridge is in stark contrast to the menu of exuberance and sensuality that their 'papist' chef serves up for them. Initially dubious about the meal and the indulgence it represents, the diners vow to remain silent

MENU

Turtle soup
– *Amontillado sherry*

Blinis with caviar and sour cream
– *Veuve Cliquot Champagne*

Quail in puff pastry with foie gras and truffle sauce
– *Clos de Vougeot Pinot Noir*

Endive salad

Rum savarin with figs and candied fruit
– *Champagne*

Cheese and fruit
– *Sauternes*

Coffee and *vieux marc*
Grande Champagne cognac

Babette's Feast.

throughout. But despite their reservations, by the end of the evening, the almost orgasmic pleasure of the food (and a not insignificant quantity of alcohol) has healed old and painful wounds and brought the community together.

Reviewing the film in the London *Evening Standard*, Alexander Walker wrote, 'The actual preparation and cooking of the repast – which took two weeks' filming – is itself a mini-film of mouth-watering finesse.'

When *Babette's Feast* opened in New York, a number of restaurants reproduced the menu as part of the publicity for the film. Many still serve it today, but usually choosing cheaper alternatives to caviar and truffles. This is understandable, as Babette could afford the feast only because she'd won 10,000 francs in the French lottery – ten times what the average Frenchman earned a

Stéphane Audran as Babette Hersant.

year in 1871. But if she wanted the very best caviar, she would have needed this kind of money. Almas caviar, which is harvested from rare albino sturgeon in Iran, is reported to be the most expensive food in the world. If you want 100g of it, you'll need to part with around £2,000.

But the power of Babette's menu doesn't come from its cost. It comes from the love, joy and skill with which she prepares it. ◈

RUM SAVARIN

SERVES 6–8

For the Rum Savarin
7g (¼oz) sachet of dried yeast
50ml (2fl oz) warm milk
200g (7oz) plain flour
3 large eggs
90g (3½oz) unsalted butter, softened, plus extra for greasing

For the syrup
330g (11½oz) sugar
500ml (18fl oz) water
zest 1 orange
4 tablespoons rum

For the garnish
4–5 fresh figs, cut into halves and quartered
200ml (7fl oz) whipping cream
50g (1¾oz) icing sugar
zest 1 orange
200g (7oz) fresh raspberries
10g (½oz) fresh mint

Note: you will need a classic style 20cm Savarin mould and piping bag for this recipe.

In a small jug, dissolve the yeast in the slightly warmed milk.

Using a cake mixer fitted with the beater attachment, beat the flour, yeast mixture and eggs for 2–3 minutes until it forms an elastic dough. If you don't have a mixer, you can also use a wooden spoon. Cover the dough with a cloth and leave in a warm place to prove for about an hour.

Preheat the oven to 200°C/180°C fan/390°F/gas mark 4 and grease the Savarin mould generously with softened butter.

Place the now proved dough back into the mixer and add the softened butter and 1 tablespoon of the sugar. Beat again for another 2 minutes before transferring the dough into a piping bag (no need to use a nozzle).

Pipe the mixture into the prepared mould, tapping the mould on the surface as you pipe to ensure any air bubbles are removed and the mixture lays flat.

Leave the cake to rise, uncovered for 30 minutes, before baking for 25–30 minutes in the preheated oven. When cooked, the cake should look golden and spring back when touched.

While the cake is cooking, make the syrup. Pour the remaining sugar, water and orange zest into a small pan and bring to a simmer for 10–15 minutes until it is slightly reduced. Then add the rum.

Remove the cake from the oven. Wait 5 minutes before turning it out onto a cooling rack and pouring over the syrup and rum mixture.

Leave to cool while you whip the cream to firm peaks with the icing sugar and orange zest.

Transfer your cooled Savarin onto a plate. Place the cream into a piping bag with a star nozzle and pipe into the centre of the Savarin, but only when you are ready to serve and the cake is completely cooled. Garnish with the figs and fresh raspberries, torn mint leaves and a dusting of icing sugar.

ATHLETES' MENU

PyeongChang Winter Olympics, 2018

On the basis that the world's finest athletes require the best possible diet to perform at their very top level, it seems strange that it was not until the 1984 Olympics in Los Angeles that organisers suggested it might be a good idea to bring in food specialists to devise the Olympians' menus.

Naturally, athletes have differing needs (as well as religious and cultural requirements, not to mention allergies/intolerances), but even at the 1996 Atlanta Games athletes were still complaining that the menu needed to include more low-fat, high-carbohydrate options. Four years later in Sydney, things had changed, not least in that the organisers actually asked the athletes what they wanted and trialled the menus at pre-Olympics training camps. In came multicultural Australian cuisine and regular changes to reduce menu fatigue. Out went peanuts.

By the time of the PyeongChang 2018 Winter Olympics, the catering had moved up to an entirely different level, with nutritionists right to the fore in the menu selection and issues such as sustainability among the key considerations. For the almost 8,000 athletes and officials, the organisers put together an 18-page menu which required the handiwork of nearly 200 chefs. They dished out about five million meals, including Kosher, halal, vegan, gluten-free and just about every national cuisine you could name.

The Korean barbecue option was especially popular, but there were also plenty of cheese choices (Edam, Swiss, Camembert, Feta, Cheddar, Bocconcini and Grana Padano), as well as nine different kinds of bread. Grilled sea bass and halibut? Tick. Kimchi? Tick. Quite a lot of pizza? Tick.

But of course it's not just the athletes who have to eat at the Olympic Games – there are an awful lot of spectators there, too. Organisers are keen to make visitors feel at home, so special menu arrangements for them are often put in

Closing ceremony of the Winter Olympics, Pyeongchang, South Korea, 2018.

place. At the 2008 Games in Beijing, all 112 official Olympic restaurants were told to take dog meat off the menu to avoid giving offence to the incomers. Restaurants around the city close to key venues were also advised to rename some of their translations, so that, for example, 'husband and wife's lung slice' became the slightly less worrying 'beef and ox tripe in chilli sauce'.

At the 2012 London Games, visitors were treated not only to a selection of international dishes but also to the very best of British cuisine, including Cornish pasties, Yorkshire puddings and bacon butties. However, there was a slight problem with the fish and chips. After some debate with official restaurant sponsor McDonald's, it was agreed that fish and chips could be sold as an entire dish, but not chips on their own, since the chain had sole rights on chips and French fries. ◈

PIXAR'S CEREAL MENU

Today

SINCE CREATING *TOY STORY* IN 1995, PIXAR STUDIOS HAVE TRANSFORMED and dominated the world of animation. Along the way they've picked up Oscars for films about fish, robots, monsters, bugs and old men trapped in grief. It's not surprising that journalists want to visit them. And it's equally understandable that they're cautious about it. When the lucky few are let in, their resulting articles range from dissertations on creativity to ponderings on technology and management structure. But most of them also talk about 'the cereal room'.

The cereal room is open all day to all employees. People are encouraged to fill their bowl from the selection of often fairly sugary treats whenever they feel the urge. Eat at your desk, eat in a screening, eat on your scooter. It's a far cry from the controlled-eating schedule of the 1950s, when everyone had to be hungry when the factory whistle blew and thirsty when the clock struck four.

Pixar isn't alone among the high-tech West Coast giants in providing its people with tasty perks. Google's offices have several restaurants, offering everything from sushi to salt beef. They have chefs waiting to stir-fry your tofu or carve you a little meat from the rare end of the joint. They even have teaching kitchens, so people can learn how to re-create their favourite work food when they get home. The catering at Facebook is so good that when the company wanted to create a massive new development in the city of Mountain View, the local restaurateurs were up in arms. In the end, the city was so worried about the damage Facebook might do to local restaurants that it only granted permission for the development on the condition that they didn't offer free food.

Some observers say that free food, like in-office gyms, laundry services and even ballet and sculpting classes, is just a way of increasing the number of hours people spend at work. Less cynical commentators say it's a way of making work more social, more collaborative and more fun. They argue that, just like better parental leave and the increasing acceptance of pets in the workplace, it makes people happier.

Pixar are really proud of their cereal culture. They've even made a film about it, which calls the cereal bar the best room in Pixar. But they do acknowledge that some of the cereals are more childhood vices than grown-up body fuel. According to the US Department of Agriculture, Cap'n Crunch is 44 per cent sugar. Kellogg's Frosted Flakes are 35 per cent sugar. But Kellogg's has done something about the sugar – they've removed the word from the product's name. Before 1983, they marketed them as Sugar Frosted Flakes. ◈

MENU

Mini Wheats

Rice Checks

Cap'n Crunch

Honey Nut Cheerios

Oats 'n' Honey Granola

Cheerios

Total

Cinnamon Toast Crunch

Cocoa Puffs

Low-fat fruit granola

Corn Pops

Frosted Flakes

Smart Start

Lucky Charms

Grape Nuts

Muesli

Cinnamon Toast Crunch

CHAPTER SIX

WAR AND PEACE

While the Duke of Wellington celebrates with a feast, soldiers try Tickler's jam in the trenches, and then a lot of beer at a reunion in Australia. There's also a trip to Korea to decode the Peace Summit menu and then back to blighty for tripe a la mode at the Café Royal.

DUKE OF WELLINGTON'S WATERLOO BANQUET

18 June 1839

A COALITION OF FORCES, LED BY THE DUKE OF WELLINGTON AND THE Prussian Field Marshal von Blücher, defeated Napoleon at Waterloo on 18 June 1815. The battle marked the end of the Napoleonic Wars and helped to establish Britain as the dominant military force in Europe.

In 1820, on the eve of the fifth anniversary of Waterloo, the Duke of Wellington held a victory banquet at his London residence, Apsley House – a home with the charismatic address 'No. 1 London'. It was primarily a reunion dinner for the officers who had fought alongside him during the campaign. The dinners became an annual event until the Duke's death in 1852, and were so popular that members of the public would queue up to watch the Duke's staff prepare the room for the night's festivities.

The most striking thing about this menu is its size. Not the quantity of food – that prize surely belongs to George IV's Coronation Banquet (see page 66) – but the number, range and complexity of dishes. To prepare just one of these demands hours of work and years of expertise. And the menu contains dozens of them. Antonin Carême's recipe for *Pain de Gibier à la Gelée*, for example, begins with instructions to roast and then purée ten rabbits and ten partridge. The purée, mixed with an almond sauce, seasoning and aspic, is then packed into ornate moulds and iced until set. Once turned out, the towering dishes are decorated with truffles, cocks' combs and tiny jelly squares in contrasting colours. These dishes were feasts for the eye as much as the tongue; presented on raised stands so guests could truly marvel at them. And many of them – jellies, pâtés, charlottes and pies – could even be sculpted into the shape of towers, cavalry and ordnance, to remind guests of their Peninsular campaign.

MENU

4 Potages Tortue *4 Printanniers*

4 Poissons

Le Turbot sauce Homard *Les Filets de Soles au Velouté*
Les Truites sauce Genevoise *La Matelotte d'Anguilles*

4 Relevees

La Poularde à la Regence *Le Jambon au Madère*
Les Filets de Boeuf à la Jardinière *La Tête de Veau en Tortue*

24 Entrees

2 Suprême de Volaille aux Truffes
2 Filets de Canetons aux Petits Pois
2 Filets de Pigeons à la Marechale
2 Cotelettes d'Agneaux à l'Italienne
2 Ris de Veau Glacé aux Asperges
2 Filets de Lapreaux à la Toulouse
2 Quenelles de Volaille à la Bechamelle
2 de Poulets à la Reine à la Chivry
2 Tendrons de Veau aux Laitues Macédoine
1 Filets de Volaille à la Orly Sauce Tomate
1 Pâte Chaud à la Financière
1 Timbale Macarony à la Milanaise
1 Casserole Pommes de Terre Blanquette de Volaille
1 Casserole au Riz à la Reine
1 d'Escaloppe de Levreaux aux Champignons

4 Rôtis

1 de Caille Bardée *1 Poularde* *1 de Caille Bardée* *1 de Levreaux piques*

4 Relèves Froids

1 Pain de Gibier à la Gelee	*1 Le Pâté de Faisan*
1 Baba au Madère	*4 Relèves Assiettes Volantes*
1 Soufflé à la Vanille	*1 La Fondue au Fromage*
1 Soufflé au Citron	*1 Le Ramequin Parmesan*

24 Entremets

2 Macédoines de Fruits	*2 Charlottes de Fraises*
2 Crème à la Vanille	*2 Gelées d'Ananas Garnies*
1 Franchounettes Meringuées	*1 Nougat de Pommes*
1 Genoises Glacées	*1 Dartois d'Abricots*
1 Bordure d'Aspic Garnie d'Oeufs de Pluviers	
	1 Les Ecrevisses au Vin de Champagne
1 Salade de Homards	*1 la Bordure d'Oeufs de Pluviers*
2 de Petits Pois à la Française	*2 d'Aricots Verts à la Maitre d'Hotel*
2 d'Artichauds à la Barigoule	*2 d'Asperges Sauce au Beurre*

Table de Côté 1er Service	*Table de Côté Second Service*
2 de Petits Vols au Vent Bechamelle	*2 Tartes de Pommes*
2 de Croquettes de Volaille au Velouté	*1 Tarte Gooseberry*
2 Hanches de Venaison	*1 Tarte Currents*
1 Roast Beef	*1 Pudding de Cabinet*
1 Selle de Mouton	*1 Gateau de Riz*
Rix au Consommé	
Merlents Frit	

The menu also contains the most celebrated of Georgian foods – turtle soup. Green turtles first arrived in Britain in the eighteenth century, when sailors kept them alive onboard ship as a source of fresh meat. But they were so delicious that they soon became a must-have item on any well-to-do table. At the height of the trade, 15,000 live turtles were being imported into Britain every year. In just a few decades, demand for turtles led to them being hunted almost to extinction. By the nineteenth century, they were so rare that only the wealthiest could afford real turtle for their soup. The less wealthy had to make do with the mock turtle (see Mrs Beeton's Dinner for 18 Persons, page 163).

The second surprising thing about a menu celebrating victory over the French, is that it's written in French. Britain's great naval hero, Lord Nelson, may have described the French as 'thieves, murderers, oppressors and infidels', but Wellington was of a different opinion. At the age of 16, then plain Arthur Wellesley, he'd enrolled in the Royal Academy of Equitation at Angers, where he became fluent in the language and fond of all things French, including the

The Waterloo Banquet, 1836

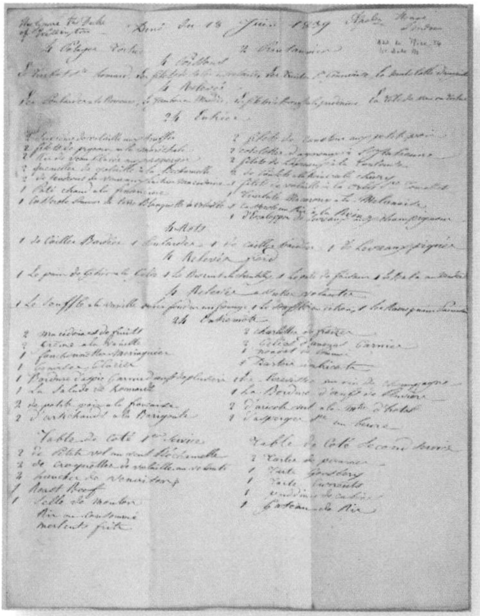

food. So, while the name of the menu's chef remains unknown, we can be fairly confident that he was born on the other side of the English Channel.

What we can be less confident about is the purpose of this 1839 menu – it may have formed part of the instructions to the kitchen, or have been a record created after the event. It certainly wouldn't have appeared at the table.

But even without a commemorative menu, no guest would leave in any doubt about the success of the Duke's campaign and his significance on the European stage. The silverware used for the dinner was the Portuguese service, given to the Duke in 1816 in recognition of his role in liberating the Iberian Peninsula. It's made from Spanish and Castilian coins, and comprises more than a thousand pieces, decorated with mythical creatures, allegorical figures and symbols of military victory. The walls of the Duke's dining room, as William Salter's 1836 painting of the banquet reveals, are adorned with works of art, many from the Spanish Royal Collection. The Duke's forces had liberated the collection from Emperor Napoleon's brother Joseph, after he fled Spain following defeat at the Battle of Victoria in 1813.

Eagle-eyed gastronomists may spot 'merlents frites' on the menu and wonder what on earth this dish is, given that the word 'merlent' doesn't seem to be a real one. Perhaps it's a misspelling of the French word 'merlan' – one which reflects the French pronunciation of the word. In which case, this dish is fried whiting.

While most of the menu is French, and the decorations Spanish and Portuguese, there are a few quintessentially English items that reflect the Duke's personal taste for British sweet treats. Guests, including the ladies, who would be invited to join the gentlemen for dessert, can choose from rice pudding, gooseberry pie and cabinet pudding. ◈

WORLD WAR ONE BRITISH SOLDIERS

1914–18

MENU

From 'Laventie', by Ivor Gurney:

Of Maconachie, Paxton, Tickler,
and Gloucester's Stephens;

Fray Bentos, Spiller and Baker, odds
and evens

Of trench food, but the everlasting
clean craving

For bread, the pure thing, blessed
beyond saving.

Composer and war poet Ivor Gurney concentrated in his verse more on the day-to day side of life in the trenches and the, admittedly few, lighter parts of the experience rather than making grand statements. His poem 'Laventie', excerpted above, is a good example, containing what probably amounts to the nearest we can come to a menu for British soldiers in the trenches of World War I.

Maconochie stew was the staple, a tinned concoction of beef, potatoes, haricot beans, turnips, onions and carrots, served to the troops since the Boer War more than a decade earlier. It was designed to be consumed hot after 30 minutes of boiling, but of necessity was often eaten cold. Hot, it was deemed to be passable at best. Cold, when the fat had congealed, it was not so popular, with the added issue that it gave soldiers appalling wind and constipation.

Maconochie was so ever-present in soldiers' lives that the word entered their slang as a term for, variously, the stomach, a telephone receiver and the Military Medal and Military Cross. Interestingly, the two villains in the 85th Field Ambulance's wartime pantomime of Dick Whittington in Macedonia were 'Count Maconochie' and 'Sir Joseph Paxton', the latter named after one of the brands of jam provided for the troops.

Tickler's jam was almost as ubiquitous as Maconochie stew. Not a firm set, it was simply poured out without the need for a knife or spoon. It came in two colours, green and red (the colour was disconcertingly unimportant as they were both plum-and-apple flavour), with the bonus that empty tins were recycled as homemade grenades known as 'Tickler's artillery'. A song of the period recounts:

Tickler's Jam! Tickler's Jam!
How I love old Tickler's Jam.
Plum and apple in one-pound pots
Sent from England in ten-ton lots.
Every night when I must sleep
I'm dreaming that I am
Forcing my way up the Dardanelles
With a pot of Tickler's Jam.

One of the problems with bread and jam or marmalade was that it was hard for men in the front line to get it into their mouths without also eating a mouthful of flies.

A century later, most of the brand names Gurney namechecks are all but forgotten, although Fray Bentos tinned pies (named after the Uruguayan town where they were originally made) are still available on supermarket shelves. Its corned/bully beef (a forerunner of the Spam® which arrived in the UK from the USA in World War II) was popular enough among soldiers for 'Fray Bentos' to become slang for something which was OK.

Not always so popular were the biscuits. A Spiller and Bakers cracker that survived the *Titanic* was sold in 2015 for just over £15,000. This kind of longevity made it useful for wartime rations (and also as dog biscuits). Biscuits produced

Clockwise from top left: bread served in front line trenches; an English soldier having a bowl of soup; soldiers on the Western Front eating to celebrate Christmas Day in a shell hole, partly occupied by the grave of a comrade.

by the official government contractor, the Quaker-run Huntley & Palmers, were so tough and dry they were potential toothbreakers if not dunked in tea or water first.

The target calorie count per soldier was around 3,500 a day, but the diet was lacking in vitamins and often fell short due to supply issues and challenges such as the German U-boat blockade. A flour shortage in 1916 meant turnips were used to make bread, causing diarrhoea, while battalion cooks (there was no Army Catering Corps until the next world war) used weeds to enhance soups. Men grew their own vegetables and went fishing to add to their rations. The soldiers' daily diet was also enhanced by the irregular arrival of food packages from home which often contained chocolate, cakes and tobacco. Harrods was one of several notable department stores which produced catalogues of food to make it easier for their customers to choose what to send out to the front.

To wash it all down there was tea, which was pleasantly familiar and masked the grotty taste of water frequently carried about in old petrol cans. There was also rum, though when this was given out it usually indicated the men were soon to go over the top…

Stew, biscuits and tea were not always the whole story. Towards the end of 'Laventie', Gurney adds:

But Laventie, most of all, I think is to soldiers
The Town itself with plane trees, and small-spa air;
And vin, rouge-blanc, chocolat, citron, grenadine:
One might buy in small delectable cafés there.

Soldiers serving in France could sometimes take advantage of *estaminets*, small impromptu cafés near the front line which provided the men with treats such as eggs and chips (these *pommes de terre frites* were called 'Bombardier Fritz'), and vin blanc, swiftly renamed as 'plonk'. ◈

1ST BATTALION AUSTRALIAN IMPERIAL FORCE ASSOCIATION SUPPER

20 October 1928

TEN YEARS AFTER THE END OF WORLD WAR I – 13 AFTER THE 1ST Australian Imperial Force (AIF) Battalion fought with distinction at Gallipoli – this reunion dinner underlines that some of the most enjoyable menus in life are the simplest. Diners, including famous Australian aviators Charles 'Smithy' Kingsford-Smith and Charles Ulm (both of the AIF, both veterans of Gallipoli), enjoyed an evening in which beer, and plenty of it, was paired with a variety of appropriate dishes, a forerunner of today's increasingly popular beer dinners.

Beer itself has long been a staple of soldiers on active duty, regarded as helpful both as a stimulant to courage and for its (arguable) medicinal qualities. Eighteenth-century British infantrymen were entitled to 5 pints (almost 3 litres) of weak beer a day, while George Washington aimed to make camp at locations close to beer supplies. Meanwhile, the 'beer and sandwiches' combo is a traditional favourite, made particularly famous in the UK under Prime Minister Harold Wilson in the 1960s and '70s as a description of the regular meetings held with trade-union leaders (journalist Andrew Marr says the first of these talks did not quite hit the spot, since the unionists preferred their bread cut rather thicker than was offered). More recently, American scientists have developed a pepperoni-and-barbecue-chicken sandwich for the army which can stay fresh, or at least last, for up to two years.

Though not technically scientists, UK bakers Greggs have also paid attention to their army clientele and trialled sausage rolls with armed forces' caterer the Navy, Army and Air Force Institutes (NAAFI).

Of the many and varied dishes from the AFI's nine-course 1928 dinner, cheese and biscuits have the most venerable military history. The English army's success in the seventeenth century in Ireland and Scotland has been at least

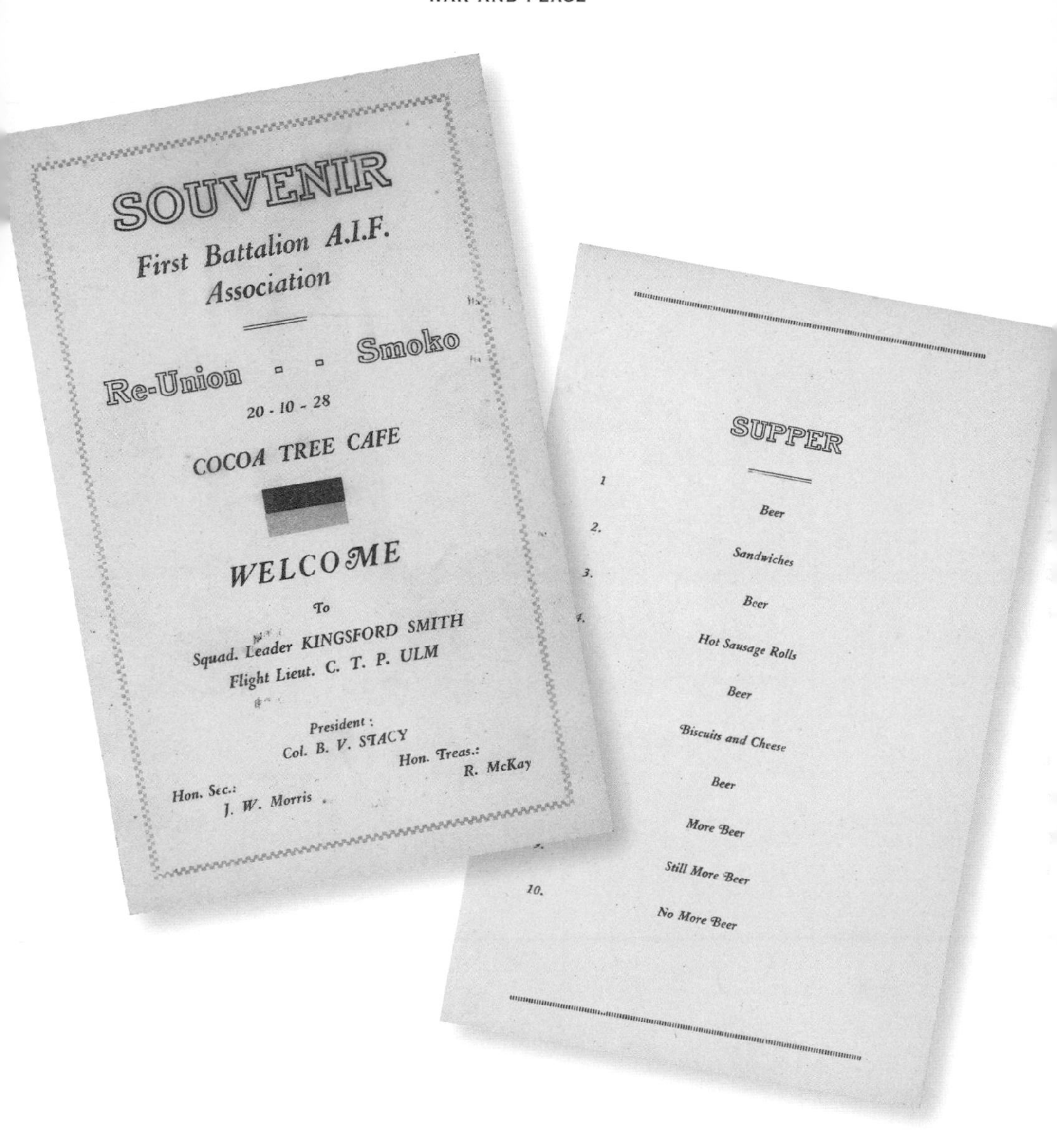

SOUVENIR

First Battalion A.I.F.
Association

Re-Union . . Smoko
20 - 10 - 28

COCOA TREE CAFE

WELCOME

To

Squad. Leader KINGSFORD SMITH
Flight Lieut. C. T. P. ULM

President :
Col. B. V. STACY

Hon. Treas.:
R. McKay

Hon. Sec.:
J. W. Morris

SUPPER

1 Beer
2. Sandwiches
3. Beer
4. Hot Sausage Rolls
Beer
Biscuits and Cheese
Beer
More Beer
Still More Beer
10. No More Beer

partly attributed to the introduction onto the ration of Cheshire cheese with biscuits which were simple, nourishing and could be stored far longer than bread before going mouldy, as well as being cheaper and easier to make. Soldiers during the American Civil War also enjoyed a weekly cheese and crackers allocation.

MENU

'Coffee' or 'tea'

'Soup'

Black bread

'Sausage'

Margarine

'Jam'

PRISONERS' DAILY 'MENU' AT AUSCHWITZ-BIRKENAU CONCENTRATION CAMP

1940–5

There were three mealtimes a day at Auschwitz, although what was served could barely be described as meals. 'Breakfast' was either a kind of grain-based coffee-substitute or 'herbal' tea that some people used to wash themselves rather than drink. At noon, there was a scarcely edible potato, flour and turnip soup – servings from the bottom of the barrel may have been lucky to get a minuscule piece of meat. Dinner was a small amount of black bread served with very low-grade sausage and perhaps a tiny piece of jam or cheese. There was no drinking water and those unlucky enough to be at the end of the food queue often received nothing. Scarcity meant that even this food became a key element in the camp's black market, swapped for clothes and other items.

From 1942, some food parcels were allowed in. Even once the SS officials had taken what they wanted, these were literally life-savers. Except for Jewish inmates and Soviet prisoners of war, who were not allowed to receive them.

Obviously, this diet lacked any kind of basic nutrition, especially bearing in mind the heavy labour many prisoners were forced to undertake. There was virtually no protein, vitamins or fats, and a calorie intake only half of what was needed, at the very best. The rations were deliberately calculated to be the minimum necessary to keep people alive: the SS officers who ran the camp did not expect prisoners to endure this regime for more than three months – they suspected those who did of stealing food. The lack of decent sustenance coupled with frequent diarrhoea caused a range of diseases such as scurvy, and ultimately brought on internal organ failure.

Research indicates that the effects of the lack of nutrition on the survivors of the camps in later life were substantial, leading to increased levels of osteoporosis and cancer as well as a range of eating-related disorders.

CAFÉ ROYAL BRASSERIE

1940–5

As the first US troops arrive in Britain, Princess Elizabeth registers for war service and *In Which We Serve* has its film première, the Café Royal in London's West End is serving up its legendary glamour and glitz, now with a side order of rationing and restraint.

A message from the Ministry of Food, restricting diners to just three courses and only one item from the starred list, gives no quarter to the elegance and etiquette of the Café Royal. Its blunt, civil service detachment wouldn't look out of place on the side of a gas mask.

The entire set menu reflects the food shortages and restrictions of wartime Britain. The only meat products available are tripe, calf's head and galantine – a dish of non-specific white meat, pressed and served in aspic. There is escalope Napolitaine, but from what animal the escalope originates is left to the diner's imagination. There's certainly no promise of traditional veal. Even the poultry and fish are from the utilitarian end of the spectrum – whiting and turkey.

Haunt of Oscar Wilde and Noël Coward, the Café Royal serves even austerity with a dash of style. 'Kippers sur toast' is proof that everything tastes better if it's written in French. And 'tripe à la mode' sounds so much more appetizing than tripe stew. When it comes to puddings though, the menu drops French chic to offer reassuringly homely treats – rhubarb and custard, and trifle.

It's odd that 'kippers sur toast' is in the dessert section. Perhaps wartime rationing meant that even Café Royal clientele were grateful for something substantial to round off their 6 shillings and sixpence meal – a modest £15 in today's money.

Not all London hotels were offering a menu as in tune with the times, though. According to the *Daily Telegraph*, in January 1941, 60 women marched into the Savoy Hotel with banners reading, 'The government says eat less, but the rich get their fill' and 'Ration the rich'. They were escorted from the premises by staff. ◈

SPECIAL NOTICE

*By order of the Ministry of Food not more than Three Courses may be served at a meal, nor may any person have at a meal more than one main dish marked * and one subsidiary dish marked ¶, or alternatively two dishes marked ¶.*

CAFÉ BRASSERIE

3 Courses only.

LUNCHEON 5/-

Hors-d'Oeuvre
or
Minestrone or Potage Fermière

-

Fried Fillet of Whiting, Tartare Sauce
or
Game Pie
or
Tripe à la Mode
or
Galantine – Russian Salad

—

Trifle
or
Rhubarb and Custard or Ice

DINNER 6/6

Hors-d'Oeuvre
or
Minestrone or Crème Garbure
Or Petites Asperges Vinaigrette

—

Filet de Sole Bonne Femme
or
Escalope Napolitaine
Or Dinde Pochée au Riz, Sauce Supreme
Or Galantine – Salade Russe

—

Mousse Glacée aux Fruits
or
Rhubarb Fool Royal or Glace Vanille
or
Kippers Sur Toast

menu continued overleaf...

PLATS DU JOUR (Ready)

Matin		**Soir**	
Potage Fermière	*1/6*	*Crème Garbure*	*1/6*
** Fried Fillet of Whiting, Sauce Tartare*	*3/6*	*Petites Asperges Vinaigrette*	*3/6*
** Tripe à la Mode*	*3/3*	** Filet de Sole Bonne Femme*	*4/-*
** Galantine, Russian Salad*	*3/6*	** Escalope Napolitaine*	*4/-*
Trifle	*2/-*	** Dinder Pochee au Riz, Sauce Supreme*	*5/6*
Rhubarb and Custard	*1/6*	** Galantine, Salade Russe*	*3/6*
Ice	*1/6*	*Mousse Glacée au Fruits*	*1/9*
		Rhubarb Fool Royal	*1/9*
		Kipper sur Toast	*2/-*

**** Game Pie 5/-***

** Crepes de Volaille 3/6 * Escalope of Chicken – Chive Potatoes 3/6*
** Calf's Head Vinaigrette 3/9 Trifle 2/-*

ORANGE SET CREAM, RHUBARB AND GINGER COMPOTE AND GINGER NUTS

SERVES 4

For the orange set cream

1½ tablespoons orange zest
75ml (2½fl oz) orange juice
1½ tablespoons caster sugar
1 egg white
250ml (9fl oz) whipping cream

For the rhubarb and ginger compote

300g (10½oz) pink rhubarb, diced into 1cm (½in) dice
2 pieces of stem ginger, chopped
2 tablespoons stem ginger syrup
70g (2½oz) caster sugar
zest 1 orange
100ml (3½fl oz) water

Ginger nuts

110g (4oz) self-raising flour
1½ teaspoons ground ginger
1 teaspoon bicarbonate of soda
40g (1½oz) caster sugar
50g (1¾oz) unsalted butter, softened
2 tablespoons golden syrup

Make the rhubarb and ginger compote. Place all the ingredients into a sauce pan except for the diced rhubarb and bring to the boil on the stove. Allow the mixture to simmer for 2 minutes before placing in the rhubarb. Cook for 3–4 minutes on a low heat before turning it off. You want the rhubarb hardly cooked and with texture. Leave the rhubarb to cool in the mixture while you make the cream.

Make the set orange cream by first combining the orange, juice, zest and the sugar into a bowl and stir until the sugar has dissolved.

In a mixing bowl, whisk the egg whites to firm peaks and set aside.

In a separate bowl, whisk the whipping cream. As it starts to thicken, drizzle in the orange and sugar mixture. Continue to whisk until you start to see stiff peaks. Finely, gently fold in the whipped egg whites. Spoon or pipe the mixture into glasses and set in the fridge for 2–3 hours.

Now you can make the ginger nuts. Preheat the oven to 200°C/180°C fan/390°F/gas mark 4 and line a baking sheet with parchment paper.

Sift all the dry ingredients except the sugar into a large mixing bowl. Add the sugar and the butter and rub together until crumbly.

Add the golden syrup and mix together until you form a firm paste.

Roll the paste into 12–16 little balls, place them onto the lined parchment and press them down slightly. Make sure to leave enough space in between each one. (It's easier to handle the paste if your hand is slightly wet).

Place the tray into the preheated oven and bake for 10–15 minutes until the biscuits have spread and have a cracked appearance. Leave to cool.

Drain the rhubarb compote slightly and spoon the cooked rhubarb onto each of your set creams. Serve with a ginger nut biscuit.

KOREAN PEACE SUMMIT

2018

GASTRODIPLOMACY IS ALL THE RAGE NOWADAYS. AS HILLARY CLINTON once remarked, 'Food is the oldest diplomatic tool.' There is even an organisation, Le Club des Chefs des Chefs, which is made up entirely of current personal chefs of a head of state and whose mission statement reads, 'If politics divides people, a good table always gathers them.'

Culinary statecraft can result in intriguing offerings. Guests at the 2012 State Dinner held by US President Barack Obama for the visit of then UK Prime Minister David Cameron were treated, in the words of the White House, to a main course which was a 'great marriage of the two countries', Bison Wellington.

For the historic peace summit between North and South Korea in 2018, symbolism was literally built into every aspect of the event, from the circular table the officials sat around (diameter 2,018mm) to the choice of filling for the 'pyeonsu' dumpling course (minced croaker and sea cucumbers from Gageodo, home town of former South Korean President Kim Dae-jung).

MENU

Mineohaesam pyeonsu

A bowl of rice

Charcoal-grilled beef

Cold salad mixed with sliced octopus

Bibimbap

Grilled John Dory

Steamed red snapper and catfish

Rösti

Naengmyeon

Mango mousse

Tea made with mushrooms

Here's why it was all chosen:

- RICE – cultivated using an eco-friendly method (the paddies are weeded by ducks) from Bongha, the village where former South Korean President Roh Moo-hyun was born (he had chaired the previous inter-Korean summit in 2007).

- BEEF – from Seosan Ranch in the central South Korean Chungcheongnam-do province, from where the founder of Hyundai, Chung Ju-yung, led a truck convoy of 1,001 'unification cows' in a peace mission to North Korea in 1998.

- OCTOPUS – caught off Tongyeong, home town of Korean-German composer and reunification campaigner Isang Yun.

- BIBIMBAP – made with rice, wild vegetables and herbs from Biha, the village where Roh Moo-hyun grew up. Bibimbap was also served to Ivanka Trump on her 2018 visit to South Korea to symbolise harmony.

- JOHN DORY – a staple fish dish in Busan, where South Korean President Moon Jae-in spent his childhood.

- RED SNAPPER AND CATFISH – the first is a freshwater fish found in both Koreas, the second is eaten during feasts in both North and South, indicating the similarities between the two.

- RÖSTI – a dish from Switzerland, where the Supreme Leader of North Korea Kim Jong Un went to school.

- NAENGMYEON – cold noodle soup, served by a North Korean restaurant based in Pyongyang, on the suggestion of President Moon Jae-in.

- MANGO MOUSSE – subtitled 'Spring of the People', this was topped with a map of a unified Korea, the whole thing encased in a hard chocolate dome which diners had to smash to get at the mousse (symbolising a warm relationship breaking through).

- TEA – the mushrooms came from the Baekdudaegan mountain range which runs from North to South Korea, representing unity.

- AND TO WASH IT ALL DOWN, some tasty Dugyeonju wine made from azalea petals and glutinous rice, and Munbae-ju liquor, which has a scent of wild pears (though no pears are used in its production), designated as Important Intangible Cultural Property No. 86–1 in South Korea, but originating from the North.

But food statecraft is just as tricky as the non-edible kind. As soon as Japanese diplomats saw the map on the mousse, they lodged a protest and demanded its removal, since it included the Dokdo Islands, which are a matter of dispute between South Korea and Japan. You can't please everybody.

North Korean leader Kim Jong-Un (left) and South Korean President Moon Jae-In (right) opening the 'Spring of the People' dessert.

CHAPTER SEVEN

ANCIENT AND CLASSICAL

SHARE A MEAL ON THE GO WITH OTZI THE ICEMAN, A SLICE OF RHINO WITH A NEANDERTHAL OR AN EGYPTIAN SET MENU THAT IS CARVED IN STONE. THEN, AFTER TRASHING THE TRANSFORMATIVE MYTH ABOUT KING MIDAS, RETURN TO ANCIENT ROME TO ENJOY SOME FLAMINGO TONGUES WHILE STARING AT THE FLOOR.

NEANDERTHAL MAN'S MENU

46,000–30,000 BC (Tuesday)

We all know that Neanderthals lived in caves, carried clubs and ate mammoth. We've seen the cartoons. And to be fair to the cartoonists, until recently, their sketches broadly reflected the evidence. Bones – including reindeer, rhino and, of course, mammoth – found in the caves where Neanderthal man lived, suggested a purely carnivorous diet. Some pre-historians even thought that the reason Neanderthal man died out and modern humans survived, was that modern humans had learned to eat their vegetables.

But recent research reveals that Neanderthal men and women had a much more varied diet than we gave them credit for.

Dr Laura Weyrich from the University of Adelaide led a study that analysed the dental plaque on the teeth of Neanderthals from Spy Cave in Belgium and El Sidrón cave in Spain. In a paper published in 2017, she reported that each plaque nugget contained DNA evidence of the food the teeth had chewed on. There's also recent research into Neanderthal faecal matter, but there's no place for that in a book about menus.

MENU

Woolly rhinoceros

Wild sheep

Mushrooms

Pine nuts

Date palms

Peas

Beans

Barley porridge

Water lilies

Tree bark

Moss

While the Belgium cave dwellers ate mainly meat – mammoth and wild sheep – the Spaniards had an almost entirely vegetarian diet – mushrooms, pine nuts, tree bark and moss. In samples from Iraq, there's evidence of beans, peas and date palms, too. It seems that those living on the cold, open plains of Northern Europe hunted. Those living in the warmer forests of Southern Europe foraged. But before we become too enamoured of our vegetarian cousin, we should bear in mind that the research revealed evidence of cannibalism in El Sidrón too.

According to Google, the 'Paleo diet' was the most searched-for diet of 2014. It limits its followers to foodstuffs that Neanderthals would have eaten – a diet devoid of processed food such as grains. But traces of starch found in Neanderthal plaque mean they might have to rethink this regime. The starch suggests, for the first time, that Neanderthals had learned to cook some of their food – water-lily tubers and barley – to get the maximum nutritional value from them.

It's not only the Neanderthals' dining that turns out to be more sophisticated than we thought. Weyrich analysed plaque from the teeth of a young male and discovered that he was suffering from a stomach virus. But the DNA evidence also revealed that he was taking medication for his condition. His plaque contained Penicillum, the mould that produces the antibiotic penicillin. It also contained poplar bark, a natural source of salicylic acid, which is an aspirin-like painkiller. ◈

OTZI THE ICEMAN'S COPPER AGE MENU

c. 3282 BC

It may sound like the menu from a pop-up restaurant in Shoreditch, but Otzi enjoyed this meal atop a glacier on the Austrian-Italian border around 5,300 years ago. A resident of the Copper Age – the rarely celebrated period between the Stone Age and its technically advanced grandchild, the Bronze Age – he belonged to a society that was turning metal into useful and pretty objects for the first time.

The menu was created by scientists at the Eurac Research Institute for Mummy Studies in Bolzano, Italy, and is based on their analysis of the mummified contents of Otzi's stomach and gut. What's striking about it is how well suited it is to the needs of someone travelling by foot in a hostile, cold environment like the Alps.

The fat content of this menu is around 50 per cent – much higher than the recommended level in a healthy modern diet. But the extreme temperatures that Otzi was living in meant he needed to take in huge amounts of calories quickly. Fat is great for that. This is something Captain Scott discovered to his cost when

attempting to reach the South Pole (see Captain Scott's Christmas Dinner, page 16).

The deer and ibex meat wasn't cooked, but traces of charcoal found in Otzi's lower intestine suggest that it may have been smoked over a fire to preserve it. And although some of it may have been eaten fresh, meat treated in this way is perfect for trekking. It's a way of preserving food hikers still rely on today.

The einkorn that Otzi ate is a form of wild wheat. Modern shoppers can order it, or one of its domesticated cousins, from health shops. While it's not possible to work out how the grain was eaten, the Eurac team agree that Otzi's last meal was 'well-balanced in terms of essential minerals required for good health'.

The two more unusual items on the menu are bracken and mushroom. While raw bracken is poisonous to humans, and not great for cattle, it's used in folk medicine as a cure for some intestinal ailments. Mushrooms are also used in a similar way. Analysis of Otzi's intestines suggests that he suffered from intestinal problems all his life, so he may have been self-medicating. However, it may just have been that in the days before Tupperware, which wasn't invented until the Plastic Age (1907–current), bracken was the most convenient wrapping for food on the go.

A statue representing Oetzi displayed at the Archaeological Museum of Bolzano, based on three-dimensional images of the skeleton created by Dutch experts Alfons and Adrie Kennis.

MENTUWOSER'S STELA: AN ANCIENT EGYPTIAN MENU FOR THE AFTERLIFE

c. 1944 BC

MENU

Meat

Bread

Onions

Squash

Honey

Beer

Wine

IT'S HARD ENOUGH PICKING OUT WHAT YOU WANT FROM THE MENU AT YOUR local pub for Sunday lunch, so imagine how fraught the decision-making process becomes when you're considering what to snack on for eternity.

This was the challenge faced by the great and the good in ancient Egypt. Their daily diets revolved around beer, bread (in his *Histories*, Herodotus mentions Luxor's sourdough variety), meat and, to a lesser extent, fish, although priests were not allowed to eat the fruits de mer. But when preparing for the life to come, the Egyptians believed that anything that was carved into stone could become 'real' in the next world. Consequently, there are many works featuring tables covered with foodstuffs for the never-ending feast, while the walls of some tombs are also decorated with recipes for bread and cakes, as well as depictions of hunting and general food preparation.

One fine example is the limestone 'stela' or grave monument made around 1944 BC for Mentuwoser, a steward who looked after livestock for the Pharaoh Senwosret I. Now on show at New York's Metropolitan Museum of Art, it shows Mentuwoser sitting down at a table, holding a napkin and preparing to choose from a menu of calf's head and leg, various sizes of bread, onions and squash, all washed down with beer served by his father. It also features that symbol of rebirth a lotus flower, a sweet-smelling adornment not to be eaten, though pleasant in wine.

Pictures of food are all very well, but the Egyptians wisely used a belt-and-braces approach and also mummified real food for the dear departed, along similar lines to the techniques they used for humans. Tutankhamun's tomb included dozens of boxes of mummified goodies, including various cuts of meat, as well as jars of honey and wine, carefully labelled with which vineyard had produced it. Food has been found in various wooden boxes carved into the shape of what was inside, such as geese.

While there was plenty of hearty grub prepared for the longest journey, nibbles were not forgotten. In 2018, archaeologists investigating the tomb of a high-ranking official called Ptahmes in the Saqqara necropolis of Memphis discovered the most ancient piece of cheese ever found, coming in at around 3,200 years old. It was a mixture of cow's milk and either sheep or goat's milk; while nobody felt quite like tasting it, experts estimate it was probably spreadable and quite acidic. ◈

Mentuwoser's limestone 'stela', or grave monument, from around 1944 BC, on show at New York's Metropolitan Museum of Art.

KING MIDAS'S FUNERAL

c. 700 BC

When archaeologists from the University of Pennsylvania entered King Midas's tomb for the first time in 1957, they were hit by a terrible smell of rancid fat. Over 2,500 years earlier, mourners had shared the funeral banquet for their king, but no one had done the washing-up.

The tomb was discovered in Gordion, now part of Turkey, and is believed to be the oldest surviving wooden building in the world. It was found 40m below the surface of the burial mound, and its contents, including the king himself, were amazingly well preserved.

At the time, it wasn't possible to analyse the drinking vessels and bowls to discover what the menu for the funeral feast had been. However, the fact that they were bronze, not gold, dispels at least one of the myths about the ancient king. But in 1999, along came Dr Patrick McGovern, who has the extraordinary title of Scientific Director of the Biomolecular Archaeology Project for Cuisine, Fermented Beverages, and Health at the University of Pennsylvania Museum. He employed modern techniques, including infrared spectrometry, gas and liquid chromatography and mass spectrometry, to unlock the washing-up's secrets.

Fatty acids and cholesterol found in the bowls suggested that the meat was goat or lamb, but other chemicals indicated that it had been roasted and deboned before it was added to the stew. There was evidence of high-protein pulses, probably lentils, along with anisic acid, which suggested that the stew was flavoured with star anise or fennel, and olive oil.

In the drinking vessels, Dr McGovern found tartaric acid, which occurs naturally only in grapes; calcium oxalate, which falls out of barley beer during the brewing process; and beeswax, which suggests that mead was also part of the brew. These are the ingredients of what the Ancient Greeks called kykeon, although Homer's description of it suggests cheese also features. It could be made as a fairly 'soft' drink. But if ergot fungus was encouraged to develop on the

MENU

Spicy lamb or goat stew
– lamb or goat marinated in wine, honey and olive oil, grilled and then stewed with lentils, star anise and fennel

Kykeon
– a wine, barley beer and honey mead cocktail flavoured with saffron

Phrygian Valley Monument, or the Midas Monument, in Eskişehir Province, Turkey.

barley before it was brewed, the result was something considerably more potent. In this stronger form, kykeon was an important ingredient in the rites of Demeter, goddess of, among other things, grain and the harvest.

Wanting to replicate Midas's feast in 2000, Dr McGovern set a challenge for microbreweries to re-create the ancient brew. Sam Calagione, of Dogfish Head Brewery in Milton, Delaware, triumphed with Midas Touch. The bitterness in the original would have come from saffron – the most expensive spice in the world – rather than hops, which were introduced to Europe only in about AD 700. But this hasn't stopped Dogfish Head winning gold medals for its modern twist on a very old recipe. It's still available online for anyone who wants to re-create their own Phrygian funeral. ◈

SLOW BRAISED LAMB WITH LENTILS, FENNEL AND A GREMOLATA CRUMB

SERVES 6

1 shoulder lamb, bone in
5 teaspoons vegetable oil
2 white onions, peeled and sliced
4 cloves garlic, peeled and chopped
2 bulbs fennel, sliced
360g (12½oz) brown lentils, dried weight, washed
2 star anise
2 bay leaves
250ml (9fl oz) white wine
500ml (18fl oz) chicken or lamb stock
salt and pepper

For the Gremolata
75g (2½oz) flat leaf parsley, chopped
2 cloves garlic, chopped
zest 2 lemons
100ml (3½fl oz) olive oil
100g (3½oz) toasted hazelnuts

Preheat the oven to 150°C/130°C fan/300°F/gas mark 2. Season the lamb shoulder well all over with salt and pepper. Place a heavy-based casserole pan with a tight-fitting lid onto the stove and turn the heat to high. Add the vegetable oil and lay in the seasoned lamb shoulder. Fry hard on all sides for 5–6 minutes until the skin is golden and browned on all sides.

Remove the lamb and wipe out the pan with a piece of kitchen towel. Add a little more vegetable oil, turn the heat to medium and add the sliced onions. Cook with a lid on for 10 minutes, stirring occasionally until the onions are soft and slightly brown. Now add the garlic and the sliced fennel along with the bay leaves, star anise and the washed lentils.

Place the lamb back into the pan, add the stock and the wine and bring to the boil. Season well with salt and pepper. When the liquid is boiling, turn off the heat and put on a lid. You can also use tin foil.

Put the pan into the preheated oven and cook for 4 hours. Check on the lamb every hour and add a little more liquid if the lentils are drying out.

Make the Gremolata by very finely chopping the parsley, garlic and hazelnuts together with a good pinch of salt. Put the chopped ingredients into a bowl and add the lemon zest and the oil olive. Season with salt and leave to one side.

After 4 hours, turn the oven up to 200°C/180°C fan/390°F/gas mark 4. Remove the lid (add a little more stock if it's drying out). Allow the lamb skin to crisp in the hot oven for 30 minutes before removing and sprinkling over the Gremolata. Serve with a green salad and crusty bread.

EMPEROR VITELLIUS'S SHIELD OF MINERVA THE PROTECTRESS

AD 69

The Romans seem to have been rather ashamed of everyday food. Despite the vast amount of literature they produced, there isn't one complete description of a typical meal. And when they did write about food or farming, they generally apologised in advance for wasting the reader's time on such a trivial matter. But while Roman writers may have neglected everyday meals, what they did record, if only to satirise the diners, were some of the most extraordinary feasts in history.

Legend has it that, when Vitellius became Emperor in AD 69, his brother celebrated his entry into Rome with a feast that included 2,000 fish and 8,000 birds. Once in power, Vitellius spent much of his time visiting terrified senators, who were expected to entertain him with a vast array of extravagant dishes. And after he'd eaten with one, he'd move on to the next. Between these meals, if he passed a shrine with an offering on it or even the bins of a country inn, he couldn't resist having a taste – even if the morsel between his fingers had been sitting in the sun for several days. It's said that his insatiable appetite was only made possible with the help of a feather. After each enormous meal he would flick the feather around his throat

Emperor Vitellius.

to make himself vomit, and then the feasting could begin again. This perhaps explains why some records refer to him as Vitellius the Glutton.

But of all the extravagant meals he indulged in, it's one of his own design that takes the prize. This selection of unlikely ingredients was served in a dish so large that Vitellius named it the Shield of Minerva, after the goddess of wisdom and warfare. Whether the tongues, roe, livers and brains were served as separate dishes or mixed together to create one big treat is unclear. Equally baffling is why anyone would think these ingredients constituted a treat at all. But perhaps it didn't matter how tasty the dish was. What mattered was what it said about the man who could demand it.

MENU

Pike livers

Pheasant brains

Peacock brains

Flamingo tongues

Lamprey roe

These ingredients would have had to travel to Rome aboard naval triremes from opposite ends of the civilised world. Together they represent Vitellius's empire on a plate. And from each of the animals, he has selected only the tiniest part – the tongue of a flamingo, the brain of a bird. Like the rock star's insistence on only blue M&Ms, it's the rarity, absurdity and indulgence of the dish that's important. This is not food as fuel for the body, but food as a demonstration of power.

Vitellius's reign lasted only eight months. But to observe his kind of behaviour today, visit any high-end restaurant in the financial district of an international city, and watch bonus-driven bankers ordering wines from the bottom of the menu, just because they can. ◈

THE HOUSE OF THE BUFFET SUPPER

Daphne, near Antioch, Early Third Century AD

ANCIENT ROME PROVIDES US WITH SOME REMARKABLE MENUS SUCH AS Vitellius's Shield of Minerva (see page 156) and Trimalchio's riotous dinner party in Gaius Petronius Arbiter's *The Satyricon*, a 12-course monster gorge that featured a bronze donkey bearing olives, a whole wild boar filled with live thrushes, and a boiled calf wearing a helmet. But not all the best menus were written down.

Floor mosaics from the period provide us with plenty of images of Bacchus-inspired heavy drinking, but also some intriguing menus, such as the well-preserved semi-circular artwork in the House of the Buffet Supper, now in the Hatay Archaeological Museum, Antakya, Turkey. The menu, as you follow it round the mosaic, is a permanent and rather luxurious one, with a boiled egg, artichoke and pork-leg starter, followed by fish, ham and chicken for the main course, and some kind of cake as dessert, all 'served' on silver platters. Around them are breads and pitchers of wine.

Of course, this doesn't necessarily mean that this was what was on offer every day for dinner. In their 2016 research study 'Food Art Does Not Reflect Reality', Brian Wansink, Anupama Mukund and Andrew Weislogel point out that art featuring meals tends rather to include foods that underline the cultural and political aspirations of the owner, as well as those chosen for their intrinsic beauty (as a side note, the researchers also show how

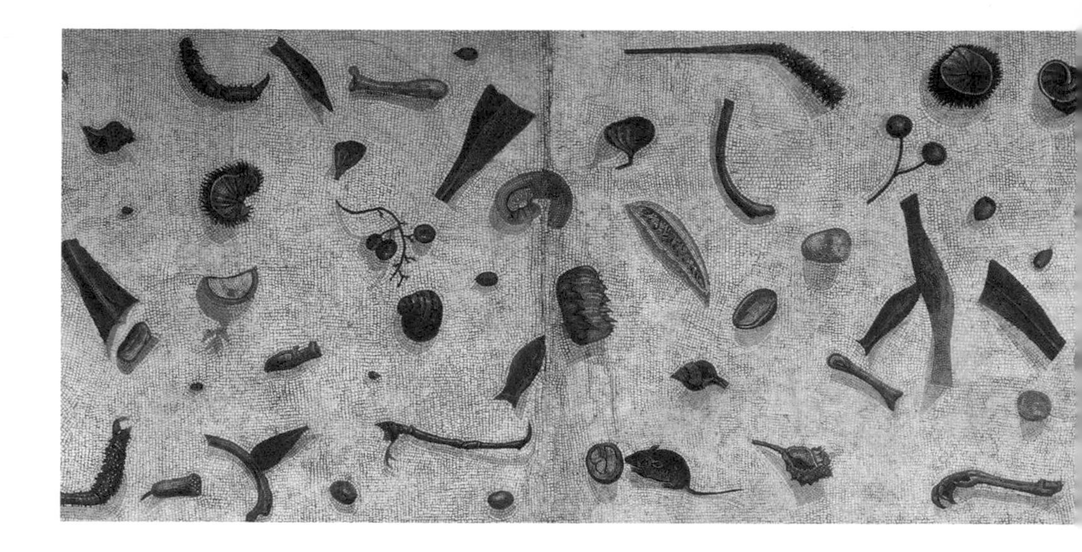

the portion and plate sizes in paintings of the Last Supper – see page 179 – have grown enormously over the last few hundred years).

The notion that these works were a self-advertisement and a way of emphasising the homeowner's high status certainly chimes with the other scenes in the House of the Buffet Supper mosaic, which feature Ganymede, the Greek gods' cupbearer, and a full bowl of wine around which the artist has pointedly included a crowd of birds.

Other examples of ancient Roman food floor mosaics include one in the famous House of the Faun in Pompeii (various fish, lobster and squid, an Aristotelian allusion connecting the owner to a cultured Alexandrian lifestyle) and the trompe l'oeil 'unswept floor' mosaic at Emperor Hadrian's villa in Tivoli, which humorously shows the leftovers from a banquet, such as crab claws, fruit pips, fish bones, nut and snail shells. ◈

Left: floor mosaic from the House of the Faun, Pompeii. Above: Asarotos oikos (unswept floor) mosaic. Roman copy of Hellenistic original by Sosos of Pergamon.

CHAPTER EIGHT

ART AND LITERATURE

While there's no doubt that Dickens was lavishly entertained at Delmonico's, the rest of these menus may never have left the page. They include a poetic wedding breakfast, explicit instructions for an inexperienced Victorian housewife, a water vole's picnic plans and some off-putting eggs. The final course is a French hero's offering to his Roman overlord.

HIAWATHA'S WEDDING FEAST

1855

First they ate the sturgeon, Nahma,
And the pike, the Maskenozha,
Caught and cooked by old Nokomis;
Then on pemmican they feasted,
Pemmican and buffalo marrow,
Haunch of deer and hump of bison,
Yellow cakes of the Mondamin,
And the wild rice of the river.

As recounted in epic trochaic tetrameter in *The Song of Hiawatha* (1855) by Henry Wadsworth Longfellow, the eponymous hero's wedding feast was quite a party. Entertainments included dancing from the handsome Yenadizze, Pau-Puk-Keewis, singing from gentle Chibiabos and story-telling from Iagoo, the great boaster. The guests themselves came in their best furs and wampum belts with beads and tassels, eating from bowls of polished white bass-wood and using black spoons made from bison horns. The food was prepared by Nokomis, Hiawatha's grandma.

The first half of the menu for the feast looks reasonably familiar to modern eyes (see Captain Scott's Christmas Dinner, First Thanksgiving Dinner and Dinner to Honour Robert Peary (Probably) Reaching the North Pole, pages 14, 16 and 182, for more on pemmican), the second half maybe a little less so.

Longfellow's poem was inspired by Native American legends and language, although one common element is omitted: that the groom and bride exchange food (usually meat and corn) rather than rings. There is still plenty of his own invention in the poem but his feast is pretty accurate, especially taking into account that the Native American population is geographically very disparate and runs to more than 500 tribes.

Buffalo bone marrow has long been a traditional Native American dish. It's very rich and fatty (a little goes a long way), but has various positive health properties, especially for the blood, and is often served on crostini or turned into soup. On modern menus it is also known as Prairie Butter. Similarly, bison hump was a widespread favourite, so much so that settlers deliberately killed bison in an attempt to starve Native Americans into capitulation – 'Every buffalo dead is an Indian gone' was one especially unpleasant mantra. There's a lot of muscle inside the hump, as this controls the animal's huge head, so a long cook on a low heat is key to making it palatable.

The health benefits of wild rice, which grows in shallow lakes and streams, have made this staple popular again in the twenty-first century. It was commonly used by Native Americans, who regard it as a sacred food. They would navigate their canoes into clumps of the plants, then gently brush the grain heads using wooden sticks known as 'knockers' to loosen and thresh the seeds into the canoe. It was then stewed, steamed or used as stuffing.

And what of the mysterious 'Yellow Cakes of the Mondamin'? Attentive readers will know that earlier in the poem Hiawatha wrestles and defeats the maize spirit Mondamin, which suggests that what was served at the feast were corn cakes.

The event enjoyed another lease of life at the beginning of the twentieth century when Sierra Leonean-English composer Samuel Coleridge-Taylor wrote a series of cantatas, the first of which was called 'Hiawatha's Wedding Feast'. Hugely popular in the first half of the century and a rival to Handel's *Messiah* in terms of performances, it then almost disappeared from the choral scene, but has happily enjoyed a renaissance in recent years. ◈

MRS BEETON'S DINNER FOR 18 PERSONS

1861

By 1850, Britain's city dwellers outnumbered their country cousins for the first time. The industrial revolution had created new urban conurbations and a new middle class to run them. These wealthy urbanites wanted to entertain their peers, compete with their neighbours and demonstrate their success. And the best way to do that was to invite people into their homes. But young wives, who had been encouraged to learn French, pianoforte and dancing in order to attract a suitable husband, didn't necessarily have the skills their mothers had when it came to running a household. And they hadn't grown up with the close connection to food production and preparation that their rural relations would have taken for granted. They needed a little help.

Enter Mrs Beeton. Isabella Beeton was a journalist, not a cook, and she didn't create any of her own recipes, preferring to borrow them uncredited from other writers. Her husband, Samuel Beeton, asked her to write household tips for his publication, *The Englishwoman's Domestic Magazine*. When Isabella was in her

BILLS OF FARE.

JANUARY.
1887. DINNER FOR 18 PERSONS.

First Course.

Mock Turtle Soup,
removed by
Cod's Head and Shoulders.

Stewed Eels. Vase of Flowers. Red Mullet.

Clear Oxtail Soup,
removed by
Fried Filleted Soles.

Entrées.

Riz de Veau aux
Tomates.

Ragoût of Lobster. Vase of Flowers. Côtelettes de Pore
à la Roverts.

Poulet à la Marengo.

Second Course.

Roast Turkey.

Pigeon Pie.

Boiled Turkey and Celery Sauce. Vase of Flowers. Boiled Ham.

Tongue, garnished.

Saddle of Mutton.

Third Course.

Charlotte à la Parisienne. Pheasants, removed by Plum-pudding.
Apricot Jam Tartlets.

Jelly.

Cream. Vase of Flowers. Cream

Jelly.

Snipes,
removed by
Pommes à la Condé.

early twenties, she produced a series of 24 monthly supplements for the magazine and, in 1861, issued them as one bound work – *The Book of Household Management*. Covering everything from boiling a ham to hiring a gardener, it was an instant hit. Later re-titled *Mrs Beeton's Book of Household Management*, it's gone through dozens of editions and is still in print today.

This winter menu reveals a new trend in the way people were dining. Traditionally, service had been '*à la français*' – meaning all the dishes were presented at the same time. But in the early nineteenth century, Russia's ambassador to Paris, Alexander Kurakin, introduced a new style of service – '*à la Russe*'. This presented dishes in a sequence of separate courses and developed into the style in most restaurants today, but it didn't really arrive in Britain until well into the nineteenth century. Mrs Beeton adopts the new fashion, dividing the meal into three courses. But old habits die hard, and some aspects of service à la française remain. She mixes sweet and savoury – serving snipe and pommes à condé (apples with a sort of rice pudding) as part of the same course, even giving instructions to replace one with the other half way through. And while modern service will eventually separate fish courses from soup courses, Mrs Beeton puts them all out together (see page 69).

The menu also shows us how important the presentation of the meal was – this may only be a suburban dinner for 18, but its purpose is to impress. Mrs Beeton indicates where the flowers should be arranged and how the dishes should be placed around them. She is also very clear when it comes to how one should eat – jelly, for instance, should be eaten with a fork, never a spoon.

The dishes themselves tell us a lot about the people around the table. The presence of mock turtle soup reminds us that this is a dinner for the middle, not the upper classes (see page 125). The recipes for this inferior alternative vary, but they all begin with the boiling of a calf's head.

Also on the menu is poulet à la Marengo. This dish was improvised by Napoleon's chef, Dunand, to celebrate his boss's victory over the Austrians at Marengo in June 1800. That a Victorian hostess could serve a dish which honours Britain's most celebrated 'enemy' shows how relations with France had changed since the Peninsular Wars and how confident the Victorians were about their new place in the world. ◈

PRESS CLUB DINNER IN HONOUR OF CHARLES DICKENS

at Delmonico's, New York, 18 April 1868

Delmonico's Restaurant on 14th Street was the first restaurant in America to offer diners an à la carte menu, a separate wine menu and arguably Eggs Benedict. Presidents such as Teddy Roosevelt regularly ate there, as did the likes of Mark Twain and Oscar Wilde, so it was a fitting venue for a special banquet in honour of the author of *A Christmas Carol,* who was about to leave for home after a exhausting reading tour of the country.

Dickens had first visited the US in 1842 but, despite the warmest possible reception, was highly critical of pretty much everything, from its intellectual property laws to the population's table manners and the custom of announcing dinner by banging an 'awful gong which shakes the very window-frames as it reverberates through the house and horribly disturbs nervous Foreigners'. American food itself he described as 'indigestible matter' (although he took an immediate fancy to sherry cobbler cocktails, so much so that he lets Martin Chuzzlewit taste one).

Charles Dickens on his American reading tour.

Food was very important to Dickens. He had experienced severe hunger as a child and wrote about its delights frequently in his novels, from a mention of chips in *A Tale of Two Cities* (see Fish and Chips, page 38) to Mr Pickwick's delight in glasses of punch. Fortunately for him, his wife Catherine was a dedicated cook and in 1851 wrote the successful recipe and menu book *What Shall We Have For Dinner?*, which quickly went through five

MENU

Huîtres sur Coquilles.

POTAGES
Consommé Sévigné. Crème d'asperges à la Dumas.

HORS-D'OEUVRE CHAUD
Timbales à la Dickens.

POISSONS
Saumon à la Victoria. Bass à l'Italienne.

Pommes de terre Nelson.

RELÈVES
Filet de boeuf à la Lucullus. Laitues braisées demi-glace.

Agneau farci à la Walter Scott. Tomates à la Reine.

ENTRÉES
Filets de brants à la Seymour.

Petits pois à l'Anglaise.

Croustades de ris de veau à la Douglas.

Quartiers d'artichauts Lyonnaise. Epinards au velouté.

Côtelettes de grouses à la Fenimore Cooper.

ENTRÉES FROIDES
Galantines à la Royale. Aspics de foie-gras.

INTERMÈDE
Sorbet à l'Américaine.

RÔTIS
Becassines. Poulets de grains truffés.

ENTREMETS SUCRÉS
Pêches à la Parisienne (chaud).

Macédoine de fruits. Muscovite a l'abricot.

Lait d'amandes rubane au chocolat. Charlotte Doria. Viennois glace à l'orange. Corbeille de biscuits Chantilly.

Gâteau Savarin au marasquin.

Glaces forme fruits Napolitaine. Parfait au Café.

PIECES MONTÉES

Temple de la Littérature.

Pavilion international.

Les armes britanniques.

Le monument de Washington.

Trophée à l'Auteur.

Colonne triomphale.

The Stars and Stripes.

La loi du destin.

Fruits. Compotes de pêches et de poires. Petits fours.

Fleurs.

Dessert.

editions. It featured imaginative 'bills of fare', dinner-party suggestions for up to 20 people including oyster curry, lobster cutlets and marmalade tarts. Dickens, who liked to end a meal with some toasted cheese, wrote the introduction under the nom de plume Sir Charles Coldstream.

On his return to New York 26 years after his first visit, Dickens very nearly decided not to attend the dinner because he was suffering with various leg and foot ailments. He was pleasantly surprised when he did turn up to find the food was as vastly improved as people's etiquette. What had changed?

In the intervening period, Delmonico's had appointed a new head chef, Charles Ranhofer, a fiercesome moustachioed figure with an impressive work ethic, and the author of the encyclopedic recipe book *The Epicurean* (1894). It was he who was responsible for the night's appropriately literary menu – stuffed lamb Walter Scott, grouse cutlets Fenimore Cooper – including a nod to the great man himself with a special timbales dish, probably made up of beets and onions. Ranhofer, who was also instrumental in popularising avocados in New York, also later came up with veal pie à la Dickens. As well as a spectacular array of food, there were impressive *pièces montées,* architectural cakes built using sugar, almond paste and meringues.

The dinner (which features in the novel *The Last Dickens* by Matthew Pearl) was men only, 204 of them at eight tables. Female journalists turned down the kind offer of being allowed to attend as long as they ate behind a curtain (see page 43). ◘

RATTY'S PICNICS

1908

EVEN IF YOU'VE NEVER READ KENNETH GRAHAME'S 1908 NOVEL *THE WIND IN THE WILLOWS*, there's a very good chance you're familiar with Mr Toad and his long-suffering friends, Badger, Ratty and Mole. Whether you met them in A. A. Milne's 1929 stage play, *Toad of Toad Hall*, or encountered them in one of the dozens of film and television adaptations, you probably know that Toad's a conceited ass with a fondness for automobiles and Ratty (a water vole, not a rat) is a good fellow, who likes nothing better than a picnic on the river.

The Edwardians were good at picnics. Getting out into the country had never been easier for townsfolk. And not just for the well-to-do. The growth of the suburban railways and the massive boom in bicycle ownership at the end of the nineteenth century meant working-class people could get out of the cities too. In 1898, the social reformer Octavia Hill, concerned by the lack of green

MENU

For Mole

Cold chicken

Cold tongue

Cold ham

Cold beef

Pickled gherkins

Salad

French rolls

Cress sandwiches

Potted meat

Ginger beer

Lemonade

Soda water

For the Wayfarer

French bread

Garlic sausage

Cheese

Flask of sunshine

spaces available to the inner-city working class, was instrumental in setting up the National Trust. So now parts of rural England were 'For Ever, For Everyone'.

But if you're to travel, you must also eat. For middle-class Edwardians like Ratty and Mole, this doesn't mean you must compromise. Whether you're visiting Calcutta or the Cotswolds, certain standards must be maintained. There are no hastily assembled sandwiches stuffed into Ratty's hamper – other than that Edwardian symbol of respectability and restraint, the cress sandwich. Instead, a selection of meats and salads is transported at whatever level of inconvenience is necessary, along with all the crockery and cutlery required. And this picnic is not excessive. Although Mole thinks it may be 'too much', Ratty replies, 'It's only what I always take on these little excursions; and the other animals are always telling me that I'm a mean beast and cut it VERY fine!'

Ratty's picnics illustrate beautifully Grahame's near-complete anthropomorphism. Beatrix Potter's Peter Rabbit, who had hit the bookstores just six years earlier, may have worn a coat, but he ate carrots and lived in fear of Mr McGregor, who towered over him like a man over a rabbit. Nothing so mammalian for Ratty and Mole. They sit down to a meal of cold chicken and beef, served with gherkins and French rolls. They're Edwardian middle-class chaps, who just happen to have tails.

The second picnic, prepared by Ratty for the Wayfarer – a seafaring rat, born in Constantinople, who has travelled to Sardinia, Venice and the Grecian Isles – doesn't make it to the stage and screen adaptations of the book. Which is a shame, because here Grahame manages to anthropomorphise even the food, which includes '...a sausage out of which the garlic sang, some cheese which lay down and cried, and a long-necked straw-covered flask wherein lay bottled sunshine shed and garnered on far Southern slopes'. ◈

DR. SEUSS'S GREEN EGGS AND HAM

1960

WRITTEN IN 1960, *GREEN EGGS AND HAM* IS THE RESULT OF A BET BETWEEN the highly successful children's author known as Dr. Seuss and his publisher, Bennett Alfred Cerf. After the publication of *The Cat in The Hat* in 1957, which contained just 236 different words, Cerf challenged Seuss to write a book using only 50. Those listed here are the only ingredients of a book which has now sold over 8 million copies.

As well as consistently making it into the Top 5 of children's picture books, it has become so much a part of American culture that when Ted Cruz wanted to filibuster the debate over the funding of Obamacare, he read the book on the floor of the Senate.

Theodor Seuss Geisel, better known as Dr. Seuss.

a
am
and
anywhere
are
be
boat
box
car
could
dark
do
eat
eggs
fox
goat
good
green
ham
here
house
I
If
In
let
like
may
me
mouse
not
on
or
rain
Sam
say
see
so
thank
that
the
them
there
they
train
tree
try
will
with
would
you

LE TOUR DE GAULE D'ASTÉRIX/ ASTERIX AND THE BANQUET

1963

THE THREE CONSTANT THEMES IN THE CARTOON ADVENTURES OF ASTERIX the Gaul are whacking Roman soldiers, arguing with his other indomitable friends, and gastronomy. But not everything Asterix and his friend Obelix come across on their travels sounds delightful. Few would be hardy enough to take on the beaver's tails in strawberry sauce or cow's hoof mould devised by Homeopathix, Impedimenta's Gallo-Roman brother in *Asterix and the Laurel Wreath*. But in general, the two warriors like to try the local delicacies – fondue in Switzerland, garum fish sauce in *Asterix and the Chariot Race* and even boiled boar in England (Obelix is not keen, although *Apicius*, a real-life first-century cookbook, features it as a favoured recipe). So it's not surprising that there is an entire adventure themed around food which doubles as a homage to the famous Tour de France cycle race.

MENU

A whole ham

Humbug sweets

Various bottles of Champagne

Sausages and meat balls

Niçoise salad

Fish stew

Sausages

Prunes

Oysters

White wine

'I'll make a bet with you,' Asterix says to General Overanxius, who is laying siege to the village of the indomitable Gauls in *Asterix and the Banquet*, first published in 1963 as *Le Tour de Gaule d'Astérix*. 'We'll go on a tour of Gaul bringing back all its regional specialities. On our return, we'll invite you to a banquet.'

On this grand culinary quest to

Obelix being served roast boar by chef Mannekenpix in The Twelve Tasks of Asterix *(1976).*

put together the ultimate Gaulish menu, Asterix and Obelix – joined by Obelix's pet Dogmatix for the first time in their adventures – take a whistle-stop tour of their own country. Unbothered by any anachronistic choices, they whizz through Lutetia (Paris, where they buy ham), Camaracum (Cambrai, humbugs), Durocortorum (Reims, Brut, sec, demi-sec and doux Champagne), Lugdunum (Lyon, sausages and quenelle meatballs), Nicae (Nice, niçoise salad), Massilia (Marseilles, a bouillabaisse fish stew – Unhygienix, the fishmonger back home, must have been pleased with this), Tolosa (Toulouse, more sausages), Aginum (Agen, prunes) and Burdigala (Bordeaux, oysters and white wine).

They don't get anything in Rotomagus (Rouen) or Divodurum (Metz) because of time pressure and Romans, thereby missing out on the local delights of cheese or cider in the former, and plums in the latter. There's also a very brief stop at Gesocribatum (Le Conquet) where, given time, they might have picked up some of the delicious local crêpes. The authors also considered other potential food and destination matches which didn't make the final cut. Arles lost out as there was already plenty of sausage, Béziers as Obelix's shopping sack was laden down with wine. However, it's a pity that there was no room for rillettes from Tours, foie gras from Périgueux, melons from Cavaillon, walnuts from Grenoble, chicken from Le Mans or vinegar from Orléans.

As always, the translations from French into English are excellent, including the Roman legionary Spongefingus, and the clever pairing of 'humbug' sweets with the French version *bêtises de Cambrai* (*bêtise* means silly mistake *en français*). This is also the first Asterix adventure in which Obelix is particularly upset at people describing him as fat or mentioning his weight.

Perhaps the most famous dish associated with Asterix is one which he and Obelix eat plentifully at home in the village and also on their journeys, but is not featured in the actual banquet – roast wild boar. Happily, there is no such omission at the Parc Asterix theme park near Paris, which serves a wild boar terrine starter, wild boar kebabs, wild boar rib platter and a boar steak burger. ◈

BOUILLABAISSE

SERVES 6

3 tablespoons extra virgin olive oil
1 white onion, sliced
1 fennel bulb, sliced
2 leeks, white and light green part, sliced
4 cloves garlic, peeled and chopped
3 plum tomatoes, chopped
200g shell on prawns
2 bay leaves
pinch saffron threads
3 tablespoons pastis or Pernod
1.5 litres fish stock
salt and white pepper
12 new potatoes, peeled and halved
300g (10½oz) clams, in shell
300g (10½oz) mussels, in shell
500g (17½oz) monkfish, cut into 6 pieces
2–3 gurnard or red mullet fillets, cut in half and de-boned
squeeze of lemon juice, to taste
30g (1oz) chopped flatleaf parsley

For the Rouille
12 thin slices of baguette
1 large garlic clove, chopped
1 roasted red pepper, peeled and deseeded
1 egg yolk
juice of half a lemon
pinch saffron
250ml (8½fl oz) olive oil, rape seed or sunflower oil
salt and pepper

First make the base of the soup. In a large, heavy-based casserole pan heat the olive oil. Add the onion, leek and fennel and sweat for 8–10 minutes until soft and translucent. Add the garlic, prawns (whole with the shells and heads), bay leaves, diced tomatoes and the saffron and cook for a further 3–4 minutes. De-glaze with the Pernod before adding the fish stock. Season with salt and pepper and bring to the boil. Once boiling, turn the heat down to a low simmer and cook for 30 minutes with a lid on.

Meanwhile, make the rouille by blending the garlic and roasted pepper in a small blender. When smooth, add the egg yolk, lemon juice and saffron and blend again. Slowly drizzle in the olive oil until it forms a stiff mayonnaise. Season with salt and pepper. Transfer to a small serving bowl, cover and put in the fridge until later.

Preheat the oven to 220°C/200°C fan/430°F/gas mark 4. Lay the sliced baguette onto a tray and drizzle with a little olive oil. Bake for 3–4 minutes per side until evenly golden. If you wish, season with a little sea salt and rub with a peeled garlic clove once cooked. Set aside for later.

Turn off the heat under the bouillabaisse and remove the bay leave. Blend with a stick blender or in a liquidiser until smooth. Pass the liquid through a sieve set over the original cooking pan to remove any bits.

Turn the heat to a low simmer and add the peeled and halved potatoes. Once ¾ of the way cooked (15 minutes or so) add the monkfish, clams and mussels. Place on the pan and simmer until the shellfish has all just about opened. Finally add the red mullet or gurnard fillets and cook for a further 3–4 minutes with a lid on.

Add a squeeze of lemon and garnish with the chopped parsley.

Serve the bouillabaisse by first evenly portioning out the fish and shellfish between 6 warmed bowls. Ladle over the soup and serve with the previously made rouille and baguette croutons on the side.

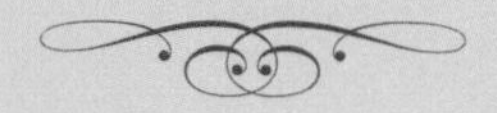

CHAPTER NINE

FAITH AND BELIEF

A menu that includes the symbolic body of a man, another that contains the actual body of a man, and one that will stretch to 75,000 diners. Then to follow, enjoy a brazenly plain menu for the 'unsuperstitious' and a distinctly Italian one for a Jesuit visiting the Big Apple.

THE LAST SUPPER

c. AD 33

It's arguably the most famous meal in history, and according to experts probably took place on Wednesday 1 April AD 33, but working out exactly what was on the menu is no easy matter.

While the meal that Jesus ate with his Apostles is the basis for the Christian Eucharist or Holy Communion, what we know for sure about its components from mentions in the Bible – specifically, the Gospels of Matthew, Mark, Luke and John, and Paul's first letter to the Corinthians – is quite limited. There was certainly unleavened bread and wine, and there are hints in Mark that there was also lamb (although in 2007 Pope Benedict XVI argued against this interpretation).

Artistic speculations in the intervening 2,000 years are not much help either. Leonardo da Vinci produced the most famous representation of the event, a mural in the refectory of the Convent of Santa Maria delle Grazie in Milan in the fifteenth century. The food is not clearly portrayed in this work, although

Detail of Da Vinci's Last Supper by Giacomo Raffaelli.

Judas does seem to be knocking over a salt cellar. Analysis by food historian John Varriano suggests that what's on this fictionalised table is in fact grilled eel with orange-slice garnish, one of Leonardo's favourite dishes. He was perhaps simply illustrating the nouvelle cuisine of his time.

The best guess of what else may have been on the menu comes from Italian archaeologists Generoso Urciuoli and Marta Berogno. Using a wide range of sources encompassing paintings and verses from the Bible (including descriptions of Herod's banquet and the wedding at Cana) combined with their own specialist gastronomic knowledge, they suggest the following as likely additions on the basis that the meal probably took place at Passover:

– *Cholent (a bean stew)*
– *Lamb*
– *Olives with hyssop (a herb with a liquoricey-minty taste)*
– *Bitter herbs and pistachios*
– *Tzir (a fish-based sauce a bit like the ubiquitous Roman garum)*
– *Charoset (a date and nut paste)*

Definitely no gefilte fish and no matzo-ball soup, both later additions to traditional Passover menus.

And all those portrayals down the centuries of the diners seated around a table? Unlikely, say Urciuoli and Berogno. It's more likely they sat around on cushions on the floor.

LANGAR, GOLDEN TEMPLE, INDIA

Fifteenth Century – Today

YOU MAY THINK IT'S TRICKY WHEN A FEW EXTRA MEMBERS OF THE FAMILY come over for Thanksgiving or Christmas Day lunch. Another one or two extra is no problem, though, for the community-kitchen organisers at the Golden Temple in Amritsar, who regularly serve 75,000 visitors a day.

The tradition of the langar – providing a free meal for anybody who wants one – is central to the Sikh faith, a deliberate effort to feed anybody regardless of age, gender, race, caste or religion (and indeed no religion). The custom was established in the fifteenth century, not merely to feed the population but as a statement for social reform. *Langars* are served in all gurdwaras, Sikh places of worship, but none deal with quite the same numbers as the Golden Temple/Sri Harmandir Sahib, which is the most sacred site in Sikhism.

To feed so many people – and the number can more than double on major festival days – takes a lot of raw ingredients, including around 15,000kg of wheat flour (they need to make about 200,000 rotis daily), 13,000kg of lentils and 5,000 litres of milk. All the food is vegetarian and is available throughout the day and night. Additional menu items are added for special occasions such as Diwali – the Hindu, Sikh and Jain Festival of Lights – but whatever the day, the food never runs out.

What is equally impressive is that all the food preparation and the consequent mountains of washing-up (each plate is washed five times before being reused) is done by around 500 volunteers, since community service is central to Sikhism. The volunteers also do the serving, piling daal and vegetables onto plates and handing rotis to locals and tourists alike, who eat as much as they like. The actual cooking is done by a paid staff of around a dozen who use enormous vats to cook the lentils over open fires. Most of the cooking is done by hand, although machinery, including a roti-maker, is used for busy periods.

Diners sit and eat together in long rows on the floor of two vast dining halls,

Some of the 75,000 guests at Golden Temple, Amritsar.

each of which has capacity for 5,000 people. Heads must be covered and footwear removed. To wash it all down there is a limitless supply of water and tea.

Though there is no charge for the meal, there is the opportunity to make a donation on leaving. ◈

MENU

Rotis

Daal

Vegetables

Kheer (rice puddng)

GOLDEN TEMPLE MARSALA DAAL WITH GREEN CHILLI AND TOMATO RELISH

SERVES 6 AS A SIDE DISH, 4 AS A MAIN COURSE OR LUNCH

For the Daal

2 tablespoons vegetable oil
1 tablespoon mustard seeds
1 teaspoon coriander seeds
1 stick cinnamon
4 cloves garlic, crushed or chopped
2 inches ginger, peeled and grated
1 green chilli, chopped with seeds if you like a bit more heat
2 teaspoons garam marsala
2 teaspoons ground cumin
6 plum tomatoes, chopped
175g (6oz) split red lentils
1.2 litres vegetable stock

For the Relish

2 plum tomatoes, deseeded and chopped
½ red onion, finely chopped
1 green chilli, finely chopped without the seeds
25g (1oz) chopped coriander
juice of 1 lime

Optional

4 tablespoons Greek or natural yoghurt
20g (¾oz) toasted flaked almonds
4 rotis

Heat the vegetable oil in a large pan or casserole dish, add the mustard seeds, coriander seeds and cinnamon stick. When the mustard seeds start popping, turn down the heat and add the ginger, garlic and chilli. Add a splash of water and cook for 1 minute, stirring all the time. Season with salt. Add the garam marsala, ground cumin and chopped tomatoes. Cook for a further 3-4 minutes before adding the lentils and the stock. Bring to the boil and set the heat to a low simmer. Stir every 5 minutes, making sure to mix the lentils so they start to break down into a puree. Cook until all the liquid has been absorbed and the lentils are tender. This will take between 25 and 30 minutes.

Make the relish by combining the ingredients listed above except for the yoghurt and almonds in a bowl and season to taste with the lime juice and salt.

Once the lentils are tender and all the stock has been absorbed turn off the heat and serve the lentils in bowls. Add a spoonful of yoghurt along with the relish onto of the daal. Add a few toasted almonds and a roti on the side if you wish.

TLACATLAOLLI, AZTEC FEAST MENU

Sixteenth Century

The Aztecs liked to ensure that certain feasts always featured the same dishes. Festivities honouring the fire god Xiuhtecuhtli revolved around deer and rabbit, while those for the god of spring Xipe Totec involved plenty of maize, the civilisation's staple. The major Xipe Totec celebration – held annually at the spring equinox – was called Tlacaxipehualiztli and the main ingredient was people.

There is some disagreement among scholars about how central cannibalism was to the Aztec diet – whether it was everyday or largely ceremonial. To whatever degree, they certainly did not believe that eating people is wrong. The remarkable Bernardino de Sahagún (1499–1590), a Franciscan friar and arguably the world's first anthropologist, devoted his life to the study of Aztec culture. He recorded that Tlacaxipehualiztli (which translates as 'flaying of men') was essentially when all prisoners, men, women and children, were killed. The warriors were the first to go in an unpleasantly one-sided gladiatorial fashion and Sahagún says that a small portion of their bodies would be added to a stew called tlacatlaolli, with maize, seasoned with salt and possibly chilli peppers. Only the family of the Aztec who had captured the prisoners was allowed to consume it.

Above is the nearest that we have to a menu for this feast, a scene from the Aztec Codex Maglabechiano, a kind of religious almanac featuring important dates and celebrations in the calendar. And plenty of gore. ◈

FIRST THANKSGIVING DINNER

September 1621

THANKSGIVING BECAME A NATIONAL HOLIDAY IN THE US ONLY IN 1863. AT the height of the Civil War, President Abraham Lincoln declared that the fourth Thursday in November should be a day for 'thanksgiving and praise'. Before then, different states had celebrated it at different times, or hadn't celebrated it at all. In his battle for the Union, Lincoln was invoking and appropriating nostalgia for a time in America's history that many people felt epitomised the spirit of the nation.

The first Thanksgiving dinner had been shared between 53 Pilgrims and 90 members of the local Wampanoag tribe in September 1621. There's no definitive record of what they ate, but it seems today's celebrations bear only a passing resemblance to the original. Not only did that first celebration take place two months earlier in the year – immediately after the harvest was gathered in – and last three days rather than one, but the menu was very different.

At the heart of today's Thanksgiving meal is a turkey. The National Turkey Federation estimates that around 45 million are eaten in America every Thanksgiving. Turkey may have been served in 1621, too. Wild turkeys were certainly plentiful in New England at the time. But duck, venison, even swan, are more likely to have been the centrepiece of the feast. Edward Winslow, an Englishman present at the first Thanksgiving, wrote to a friend:

> *...our governor sent four men on fowling, so that we might after a special manner rejoice together after we had gathered the fruit of our labors. They four in one day killed as much fowl as, with a little help beside, served the company almost a week...and they went out and killed five deer, which they brought to the plantation and bestowed on our governor, and upon the captain and others.*

Mashed potato was certainly not on the menu in 1621. Although potatoes originated in South America, and had been enjoyed as a delicacy in Europe since the 1570s, they hadn't yet made the return trip to North America. The carbohydrate on offer would have been corn. This is still part of today's feast, but in 1621 it wouldn't have been served on the cob. The kernels would have been stripped from the cob and pounded into a thick porridge, or turned

The first Thanksgiving 1621, Jean Leon Gerome Ferris

into corn bread to accompany the meat.

Pumpkins may have been on the table, too, but pumpkin pie certainly wouldn't have been. The Pilgrims didn't have the butter or wheat to make pastry – and they didn't have an oven, either.

Finally, the cranberries. As well as eating them as a fruit and turning them into cakes, the Wampanoag pounded cranberries into a paste and mixed them with dried deer meat and tallow to make pemmican – a superfood that could be safely stored for months (see Captain Scott's Christmas Dinner, page 16). Although we don't know for certain the role cranberries played in the Thanksgiving feast, we do know that the Pilgrims didn't have the sugar needed to turn them into the sticky jelly that is served today. There's no record of cranberries being boiled with sugar for another 50 years.

One of the things that the Pilgrims probably did eat at the feast was seafood – lobsters, eels and mussels were all in plentiful supply off the coasts around the Plymouth Colony. While still considered a delicacy in America, these dishes are no longer part of the Thanksgiving tradition. It may be that the desire for a meal that unified the nation – as reflected in Lincoln's declaration – is the reason for this. The foods that remain at the heart of the feast are those that the whole country can get access to. Lobsters may be plentiful in Maine, but they're rare in Colorado. ◈

THIRTEEN CLUB'S 257TH REGULAR DINNER MENU

New York, 13 December 1906

THE THIRTEEN CLUB WAS ESTABLISHED IN NEW YORK IN THE 1880S. ITS mission was to challenge the superstitions surrounding the number 13: specifically the belief that if 13 people dined together, one of them would die within the year. This belief probably had its origins in the Last Supper, but by 1911, fear of the number 13 had its own name – triskaidekaphobia.

The club's dinners usually comprised 13 courses, were often held on the 13th of the month, and each table would seat 13 guests. It may have been eccentric, but the club attracted five presidents as honorary members, including Theodore Roosevelt. This particular dinner was held in Little Hungary, a restaurant on East Houston Street, known at the time as Goulash Row. Sadly long gone, it was at the time one of the most famous restaurants in New York.

But this menu also sets out to debunk another myth – that a great menu has to be written in French. By the end of the nineteenth century, American industry was taking over the world and American confidence was rising with the Dow Jones. Philanthropists and politicians were trying to simplify American English and celebrate their own culture. Here, only parfait and café have slipped through the net. It's a menu that sticks its tongue out at dining pomposity – the fish is 'ordinary', the potatoes 'common'. The battle still rages on today. We're regularly offered cheese boards that have been 'curated', duck breasts that 'nestle' onto something 'hand-cooked', and virtually everything is 'artisanal'. Of course, the bread is 'oven baked', where else would you bake bread? ◈

IN "LITTLE HUNGARY"

257TH REGULAR DINNER

SIMPLIFED DINING

I	Just Oysters
II	Simple Relishes
III	Plain Soup
IV	Ordinary Fish, Common Potatoes
V	Mere Smoked Tongue
VI	French Peas, simplified by American raising
VII	Only Duck
VIII	Lettuce Salad, nothing simpler
IX	Café Parfait, much simpler than it seems
X	Fancy Cakes, pure and simple
XI	Simply Cheese and Crackers
XII	Black Coffee, milk omitted for simplification
XIII	Hungarian Wine, only this and nothing more

8

POPE FRANCIS'S NEW YORK DINNER

24 September 2015

When Queen Elizabeth II entertained Chinese President Xi Jingping in 2015, the menu included Scottish venison. When Xi Jingping entertained President Trump in 2018, Kung Pao Chicken and Grouper Fillets in Hot Chilli Oil were on the menu. It's understandable that a host might want to share a little of their national cuisine with their guest. But when the Pope dines in New York, everything is Italian – apart from the lobsters, which come from Maine.

All the Pope's meals during his visit to New York were prepared by a team of chefs led by Lidia Bastianich and Angelo Vivilo. Bastianich, a Croatian Italian who arrived in New York in 1958 as a refugee from Yugoslavia, is an old hand at preparing meals fit for a pope – she cooked for Benedict XVI when he visited the city in 2008.

The menu is a rich mix of shellfish, pasta and dairy products. Burrata cheese is made from mozzarella stuffed with curds and cream, just in case plain old mozzarella isn't soft and unctuous enough for you. The veal is cooked in a 'woodman's sauce' of mushrooms, pancetta and cream. Even the capon soup is enriched with tiny ravioli stuffed with parmesan.

The menu is a million miles from Pope Francis's usual dining habits. The first ever Jesuit pope, who even after becoming a cardinal preferred to carry his own bags and travel on public transport, Francis is reported to favour simple meals – skinless chicken, fruit and salad – which he often cooks for himself. His Jesuit rules even encourage him to fill up on bread before a meal, so he's less likely to be tempted by the indulgent foods on offer.

But while not Jesuit in its simplicity, the New York menu is a far cry from the most indulgent of papal banquets. The ingredients needed for the coronation banquet of Pope Clement VI in 1342, for instance, included more than 3 tonnes of almonds, 1,000 sheep and 118 oxen. There were also more than 50,000 tarts

Painting of Pope Francis on a building, New York 2015.

on offer, which is a lot even when you do have 10,000 guests. But perhaps the most notorious of papal banquets is the one allegedly held by Cesare Borgia, son of Pope Alexander VI, in 1501. Known as the Chestnut Banquet, the evening is said to have concluded with 'fifty honest prostitutes' crawling naked on the floor in an attempt to collect chestnuts that had been scattered there by the guests. Papal Master of Ceremonies Johann Burchard wrote in his diary that prizes of silk tunics and berets were awarded to those 'who could perform the act most often with the courtesans'. ◊

MENU

Caprese di Astice e Burrata
– tomato, burrata cheese and lobster salad

wine
– Vespa Bianco Bastianich 2013

Brodo di Cappone con Anolini
– capon soup with raviolini

Medaglioni di Vitello alla Boscaiola
– veal medallions Boscaiola

wine
– Vespa Rosso Bastianich 2010

Sorbetto di Uva Fragola con 'Torta degli Angeli'
– sorbet of strawberry grapes with angel-food cake

wine
– Prosecco Flor

CHAPTER TEN

PRISONS AND INSTITUTIONS

Some diners have little or no say on what they eat or where they eat it. Large portions of apartheid are on the menu at Robben Island. The condemned man has a choice and a budget in Florida. Schoolchildren are served what's good for them until market forces take over, and bread and beer are the staples in a Leeds workhouse.

LADY LANE WORKHOUSE MENU

Leeds, October 1726

The eighteenth century was a boom time for workhouses. Around two thousand were up and running by the 1770s, providing a 'home' for around 100,000 people who were unable to support themselves. There were 90 in London, housing up to 2 per cent of the city's population. A lot of hungry mouths to feed.

The world's most famous workhouse menu is also one of the most unappealing. Oliver Twist could look forward to three meals of gruel a day, two onions a week and half a bread roll on Sunday. Dickens's version of the workhouse diet was obviously entirely unsuitable for a small boy and guaranteed some combination of scurvy, rickets and beriberi. However, nutritionists argue that the actual menus were somewhat better and just about sufficiently nourishing for the real-life Olivers (assuming the quantities were received unadulterated...).

Of course it was still pretty grim. Rats were not always kept away from food as much as most people would have preferred. Likewise beetles. Bread and beer

	Breakfast	**Dinner**	**Supper**
Sunday	Bread and beer	Beef and broth	Milk porridge
Monday	Beef broth	Rice milk	Milk porridge
Tuesday	Milk porridge	Plum puddings	Bread and beer
Wednesday	Bread and cheese	Beef broth	Milk porridge
Thursday	Beef broth	Potatoes	Bread and cheese
Friday	Bread and beer	Rice milk	Milk porridge
Saturday	Water porridge with treacle	Pease porridge	Bread and beer

Top: St Pancras Workhouse, London; Bottom: Marylebone Workhouse, London.

were constants on all menus, which were usually rotated on a weekly basis. But workhouses devised their own offerings, so they differed greatly, and some even grew food themselves during hard times such as the Irish potato famine, or brewed their own ale. Gruel, too, was a mainstay. An 1847 recipe from Aylsham Workhouse in Norfolk is succinct: 'Half an ounce of oatmeal per pint of water. Boil it.' Meat was usually beef or mutton.

There was also official help at hand to improve the meals. In 1836 the Poor Law Commission handed out half a dozen diet recommendations for workhouse cooks, and at the start of the twentieth century workhouse diets were analysed in depth. The result was a special Workhouse Manual, sent to all workhouse cooks in 1901, which contained 50 recipes. These included shepherd's pie and roly-poly pudding as well as cookery tips such as the advice to boil all food instead of roasting it to save money. And over time, more milk and sugar were added.

Menus were changed only for special occasions: a hot cross bun (one per person) was often added on Good Friday. The 1,661 adult and child residents of St Marylebone Workhouse on Christmas Day 1840 each enjoyed about 170g of roast beef, 450g of potatoes and plum pudding, 600ml of porter and about 100g of sugar, tobacco and snuff, with an evening treat of oranges, apples and sweetmeats.

Portions were carefully monitored and adjusted depending on your gender and status. In his excellent *The Workhouse Cookbook*, Peter Higginbotham details the many classes – and consequent meals/portions – into which residents were divided, ranging from men not employed in work (Class 1) through women to children of varying ages and finally those on sick diets (Class 8).

The bigger workhouses had seating in rows, all facing forwards, and separate areas for men and women. Failing that, residents were served at various sittings to keep the sexes apart. Breakfast was usually at 9 a.m. under the eye of the workhouse's Master who ensured order, followed by dinner at 1 p.m. – the main meal of the day – then supper at 6 p.m. In between meals, everybody worked.

Although we think of workhouses as a Dickensian phenomenon, they lasted well into the twentieth century – officially abolished in 1930, but continuing in some form under county council control as the renamed Public Assistance Institutions until World War II. ◈

PERFECT SLOW COOKED PORRIDGE WITH STEWED APPLES

SERVES 3-4

For the porridge
150g (5¼oz) pinhead oatmeal
500ml (18fl oz) milk or water
½ teaspoon cinnamon

For the stewed apples
1 large or 2 small cooking apples
1 teaspoon vanilla paste or 1 teaspoon cinnamon
zest 1 orange
2 tablespoons good quality runny honey

To serve
flax, pumpkin or sunflower seeds

For the best result, soak the oats overnight. Cover with half the milk (250 ml) and place in the fridge, covered.

Peel the cooking apples and slice. Put the slices into a pan along with the vanilla or cinnamon, the orange zest and a splash of water. Cook low and slow until the apples start to break down. Use a wooden spoon to help the process. Once you are happy with the texture (I like them almost puréed) remove the pan from the heat and add honey to taste.

Pour the soaked oats into a heavy-based pan and add the remaining 250 ml of milk and the cinammon. Slowly bring the porridge to the boil and stir continuously for 20 minutes on a very low heat. This will produce a really thick and creamy porridge.

Once cooked, serve with the stewed apples and a drizzle more honey. Add a few flax seeds, pumpkin seeds or sunflower seeds for texture if you wish.

SCHOOL DINNER MENU

late 1940s

Rab Butler's 1944 Education Act was a beacon of hope. People were hungry for social change and the government needed to show them a better future. But with World War II still going on, government resources were limited. The Act is a miraculous amalgam of ambition and thrift. It raised the school leaving age to 15, instead of the more ambitious 16 that Butler favoured. It reduced the Church's influence on education without losing its financial support. And it made it compulsory for Education Authorities to offer school dinners, but made them free only for pupils who couldn't afford to pay.

This menu from the late 1940s embodies the Act in two courses. While it's fairly basic, and the ingredients relatively cheap, it provides one third of a child's daily nutritional needs as laid down by the Department for Health. The new Act established this as a criterion that all school dinners had to meet. For the next 30 years, children would balk at the skin on the custard and turn their nose up at the diced turnip, but their dinner ladies knew it was good for them. This menu even offers a choice of two puddings, giving children a rare sweet treat at a time when sugar was still on the ration. In 1980, Margaret Thatcher's Conservative government removed the need for school dinners to meet any nutritional

requirements. It also removed the need for meals to be offered for a set price. This paved the way for the burger, chips and twizzler menu that would dominate school dinners for the next three decades.

The Huntley Film Archives hold a documentary of school dinners being prepared in the 1940s. While the narrator is more clipped and perky than a Noël Coward tribute band, they talk throughout of 'dinners', not 'lunches'. The word reminds us that school meals were introduced to tackle malnutrition and disease in Britain's industrial cities, where dinner is served by dinner ladies in the middle of the day and children go home to tea – not dinner.

By 1951, nearly half of Britain's schoolchildren were having a school dinner. This popularity was partly due to the fact that, while many foods remained rationed well into the 1950s, school dinners were 'off ration'. So having a meal at school helped to stretch out a family's precious allowance of cheese, meat and eggs. Those who didn't qualify for free school dinners paid just sevenpence a day for them, the equivalent of around 95 pence today.

The campaign for school meals had started over 50 years before the 1944 Act. At the end of the nineteenth century, many charities, often driven by concerned teachers, began feeding children in their schools. But the meal was as likely to be breakfast as dinner – porridge with milk and treacle, bread and margarine. The health of poor children in Britain's industrial cities was shocking. In 1899, the army found that around one third of the young men volunteering for the Boer War were too small, undernourished or ill to fight.

In 1904, socialist reformer and campaigner Margaret McMillan and Labour MP Fred Jowett persuaded Bradford's Education Committee to begin offering free school meals. Technically illegal, this fuelled a campaign that would lead to the 1906 School Meals Act. This made it possible, but not compulsory, for education authorities to offer free school meals. And take-up was poor: at the start of World War II, only half the country's education authorities had adopted the scheme. It was the 1944 Act that really addressed the nutritional needs of Britain's schoolchildren.

But if we really want to offer our children the most nourishing of lunches, perhaps we should take a leaf out of the French school menu. They offer their children a four-course midday meal, which might typically include a cucumber salad with crème fraîche, followed by veal sautéed in olives and broccoli, then some goat's cheese and finally a sweet treat, like caramel semolina cake. After all this, the rate of obesity amongst schoolchildren in France is still much lower than in the UK. ◈

Children at Downhills Junior School in Tottenham line up for their midday meal.

6. <u>DIFFERANCES BETWEEN B AND C DIETS:</u>

B - Coloureds/Asiatics	C - Bantus
Mealie meal 6oz - breakfast	Mealie meal 12oz: Breakfast - 6oz Supper - 6oz
Bread: 4oz lunch & 4oz supper	Puzamandla - lunch
Fat: 1oz daily per person	Fat ½oz per person daily
Mealie rice or samp	Mealies
Meat: 6oz per person	Meat 5oz per person
Jam/Syrup: 1oz per person daily	No jam/syrup
Sugar: 2oz	Sugar 1½oz
Coffee: Breakfast - ⅛oz Supper ⅛oz	Coffee: breakfast ~~1½oz~~ 1/5

ROBBEN ISLAND MENU

1960s

Robben Island lies around 8km offshore from Cape Town. A former leper colony, it became a prison in the nineteenth century and a naval base during World War II. In 1959 it became a prison again. This time exclusively for non-white, mainly political prisoners.

Like the rest of apartheid South Africa's systems, the 'menu' divides prisoners according to their race – 'Coloureds/Asiatics' and 'Bantus' – a politicised and offensive word that the authorities used to describe any black person. The amount, type and nutritional value of the food prisoners were given depended entirely on the racial category they fell into.

Black inmates were given smaller amounts of high-energy foods – fats, meats and sugars – than other prisoners, and no jam at all. The bulk of their diet was made up of mielie meal, a maize flour that can be mixed with water to create either a smooth porridge or a thicker paste, called pap. In the middle of the day, black prisoners were also served puzamandla, a maize-based protein drink, enriched with yeast. However, one ex-inmate, who later guided tourists around the island, said they were given so little of the puzamandla powder that it barely changed the colour of the water. In 2002, Billy Nair, a South African MP who had been an inmate at Robben Island, said, 'Generally speaking the food was just to keep you alive...'

Around a third of those incarcerated were there for political crimes, mainly sabotage, the definition of which widened in 1962 to include striking, trade-union activity and the writing of slogans on walls. Future South African Presidents Nelson Mandela and Jacob Zuma, as well as Robert Sobukwe, founder of the Pan Africanist Congress movement, all served time there. The quarry in which they spent their day – and which would have sapped the strength of men consuming four times the number of calories – became the unofficial university in which prisoners educated each other in politics, literature and history. ◈

LAST MEAL OF A CONDEMNED PRISONER IN FLORIDA STATE PRISON

24 January 1989

Ted Bundy was found guilty of rape, necrophilia, prison escape and 35 counts of murder. He was executed in Florida State Prison on 24 January 1989. He didn't request a last meal, so the prison served him their standard offering for a condemned prisoner. It couldn't be a more American menu. It's not just that it's steak and eggs; it's that the eggs are served 'over easy' – fried on both sides, but with the yolk still runny. Bundy ate none of it.

Popular mythology tells us that prisoners can request whatever food they want for their last meal. In fact, the 31 US states that still have the death penalty all have individual rules and restrictions for what a prisoner can eat.

In Virginia the prisoner can choose any items from the prison's 28-day menu cycle. Teresa Lewis – executed in 2010 for murdering her husband and his son – went for fried chicken, peas with butter, apple pie and a Dr Pepper.

Her choice of fried chicken is a popular one. Very few prisoners order exotic and extravagant dishes, opting instead for high-fat, high-salt, high-sugar comfort food. And fried chicken is top of the list. John Wayne Gacy, who was executed in 1994 for rape and 33 counts of murder, asked for a bucket of original-recipe KFC and fries, along with shrimps and strawberries. Before prison, he'd managed three KFC restaurants. Rainey Bethea, the last person to be publicly executed in the US, also asked for a meal of fried chicken, before he was hanged in 1936. In Florida, prisoners can order meals from local restaurants, but they have a maximum spend of $40. In Oklahoma, the budget is less generous – $15.

In Texas, which carries out more executions than any other state, prisoners haven't been allowed to choose their final meal since Lawrence Russell Brewer's extraordinary request in 2011. The white supremacist, sentenced to death for the racially motivated murder of James Bird Jr, ordered two chicken steaks, a triple-meat bacon cheeseburger, a cheese omelette, a large bowl of fried okra with ketchup, a pound of barbecued meat with half a loaf of white bread, three fajitas, a meat-lover's pizza, a pint of Blue Bell vanilla ice cream, a slab of peanut-butter fudge with crushed peanuts and three root beers. According to prison authorities, he ate none of it. Senator John Whitmire, Chairman of the Senate Criminal Justice Committee, wrote that 'It is extremely inappropriate to give a person sentenced to death such a privilege', and one 'which the perpetrator did not provide to their victim'.

Not all requests are so extravagant. Timothy McVeigh, responsible for the 1995 Oklahoma City bombing that caused the death of 168 people, asked for two pints of mint choc chip ice cream.

But perhaps the most eloquent and understated request came from Victor Feguer, who was hanged in Iowa in 1963. He asked for a single olive with the pit in. The pit was later found in his jacket pocket.

Alcohol isn't permitted as part of a last meal in the US. But before his execution in Israel in 1962, former Nazi Adolf Eichmann asked for a bottle of red wine from the Carmel winery. The wine was served with the prison's ordinary menu of cheese, bread, olives and tea. Some reports say he refused the food, but he drank about half the bottle of wine.

CHAPTER ELEVEN

WEIRD AND WONDERFUL

Carp and lobster, cats and rats, and protected songbirds are all available on these menus. There's also one just for man's best friend, one you can actually eat, and one that probably comes flat-packed.

SAMUEL PEPYS'S 'STONE' FEAST

1663

THANKS TO HIS REMARKABLE DIARIES, WE KNOW THAT SAMUEL PEPYS LIKED his food. Barely a day goes by in the ten years of his daily chronicles of the 1660s in which he does not mention what he had to eat and drink. He records his slight concern about downing a pint of orange juice, the potentially lethal dangers of eating cucumbers, and his delight in a decent venison pasty (these were much larger in his day, the thick pastry keeping them safe-ish to eat for several months – he must have really found pleasure in his pasties, as he mentions them 50 times). He famously even buried his parmesan cheese to ensure it escaped the flames of the Great Fire of London in 1666.

There was one day of the year when he was especially keen to put together a decent menu. On 26 March 1658, Pepys had a massive bladder stone removed. It was a dangerous operation as well as a horribly painful one (his surgeon gave him a bottle of brandy to drink beforehand to numb the agony – the stone was the size of a tennis ball) and to give thanks for its success he gave a special anniversary dinner on or about the same date each year to celebrate. He called them his 'stone feasts'.

Listed right is his offering for 1663, which also included 'good wine of several sorts'. Like many of the meals he describes, it's a little lacking in the vegetable department – this

MENU

Fricassée of rabbits and chicken

Leg of boiled mutton

Three carps

Side of lamb

Roasted pigeons

Four lobsters

Three tarts

Lamprey pie

Anchovies

may have contributed to the bladder stone in the first place, though in later years he does show some interest in salads, probably partly because they were becoming fashionable and he liked to be up with the zeitgeist. Indeed, while he was a devotee of English cooking, the diary indicates his growing interest in French cuisine and customs, such as using forks rather than just your fingers.

Here's what was on the menu for 1662:

'A brace of stewed carps, six roasted chickens, and a jowl of salmon, hot, for the first course; a tanzy and two neats' [cows] tongues, and cheese the second; and were very merry all the afternoon, talking and singing and piping upon the flageolet.'

Pepys's interest in food was also reflected in his library, which is available to researchers at Magdalene College, Cambridge. It contains several cookbooks and pamphlets from the 1680s, including the anonymous 'Gentlewoman's Delight in Cookery'. However, Pepys barely did any cooking himself, and these were probably more of scientific interest to him in terms of how his meals were prepared, rather than wedged in place next to the cooker while he was rustling up his favourite oyster dish.

Pepys stopped making diary entries when his eyesight worsened in May 1669, and there is no indication of stone feasts beyond this date, but it seems likely that he kept the joyful revels going up until his death in 1703. ◆

SIEGE OF PARIS

Christmas Day, 1870

IT WAS NOT SHAPING UP TO BE A GREAT CHRISTMAS for PARISIANS IN 1870. War against Prussia was going badly, their city had been under siege since September and, even worse, they were running low on food. Very low.

Citizens were forced to improvise. They began to eat every animal in the city, starting with horse meat (more than 65,000 horses were consumed over the four-month communal incarceration) and, when that ran low, dogs, cats and rats – a rather gamey acquired taste – all started to appear regularly on restaurant menus. English journalist Albert Vandam mentions in his book *An Englishman in Paris* (1892) that as well as rat salami, people were eating begonias.

American doctor Robert Sibbet, trapped in Paris, wrote about a shop he noticed on rue de Rochechourat on 12 November:

'On the right of the stall are several large dogs neatly dressed, one hanging by the neck, others by the heels. Next to these are several large cats, also very neatly dressed, and the butcher's wife is making an effort to sell a pound or two of the meat to an aged woman who has ventured near enough to inquire the price. On the left of the stall there is a dozen or more of rats stretched upon a tray and a young woman, half veiled, is timidly approaching them with a little girl at her side.'

He adds that a goldfish now costs four dollars and that 'the epicureans of Paris have now an opportunity, as they never had before, to indulge their tastes for novelties.' Indeed they did. Because when things were looking especially grim, they started to eat the zoo. Novelist Victor Hugo was among those whose enjoyment of mealtimes took a hit. 'Yesterday we ate some stag; the day before we partook of bear; and the two days previous we fared on antelopes.' Nothing was sacred except the lions and tigers (too dangerous), monkeys (too human) and hippos (too… well, how do you cook a hippo?).

In particular it was the restaurateurs who started to innovate. This is the menu for 25 December at the iconic restaurant Voisin, rue Saint-Honoré, devised by head chef Alexandre Étienne Choron. It was Choron who bought the zoo's two elephants Castor and Pollux, and served elephant's trunk as well as elephant bourguignon. These are the key parts of his menu decoded:

Hors-d'Oevure
Tête d'âne farcie [Stuffed donkey head]

Potages
Consommé d'éléphant [Elephant soup]

Entrées
Le chameau rôti à l'Anglaise [Roast camel]
Le civet de Kangourou [Kangaroo stew]
Côtes d'ours rôties sauce poivrade [Bear chops]

Rots
Cuissot de loup, sauce chevreuil [Wolf haunch in deer sauce]
Le chat flanqué de rats [Cat fringed with rats]
La terrine d'antilope aux truffes [Antelope terrine]

Anti-Semite, anti-feminist and anti-homosexual legislator and English politician Henry Labouchère, in Paris at the time, recorded that 'I had a slice of Pollux for dinner… It was tough, coarse, and oily, and I do not recommend English families to eat elephant as long as they can get beef or mutton.' He also discusses eating a slice of spaniel. Some things didn't change, though. Choron's wine choice for the menu included Mouton Rothschild 1846 and Romanée-Conti 1858, while for dessert there was the reassuringly familiar Fromage de Gruyère.

When the Germans were finally victorious in January 1871, they immediately let large food trains into the cities, and there were major donations from the USA and Britain as well. For some it was too late. 'February 13. The domestic animals, the companions of man, have all disappeared,' wrote Robert Sibbet. 'I have not seen a living dog in a month – not even a poodle.' ◈

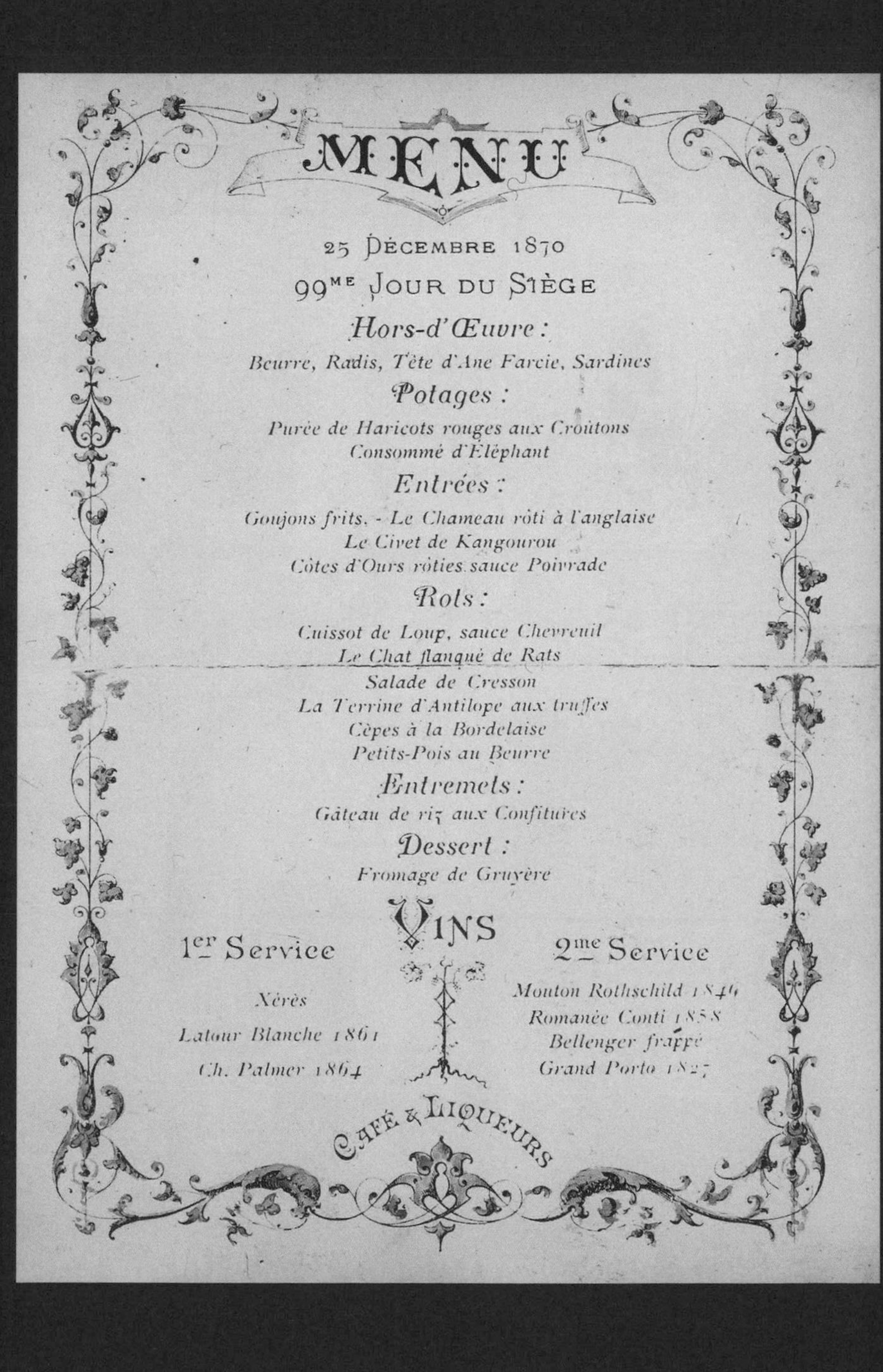

MENU

25 Décembre 1870

99me Jour du Siège

Hors-d'Œuvre :

Beurre, Radis, Tête d'Ane Farcie, Sardines

Potages :

Purée de Haricots rouges aux Croûtons
Consommé d'Éléphant

Entrées :

Goujons frits. - Le Chameau rôti à l'anglaise
Le Civet de Kangourou
Côtes d'Ours rôties sauce Poivrade

Rots :

Cuissot de Loup, sauce Chevreuil
Le Chat flanqué de Rats
Salade de Cresson
La Terrine d'Antilope aux truffes
Cèpes à la Bordelaise
Petits-Pois au Beurre

Entremets :

Gâteau de riz aux Confitures

Dessert :

Fromage de Gruyère

VINS

1er Service

Xérès
Latour Blanche 1861
Ch. Palmer 1864

2me Service

Mouton Rothschild 1846
Romanée Conti 1858
Bellenger frappé
Grand Porto 1827

Café & Liqueurs

NOBEL BANQUET MENU

1947

WHETHER IT'S IN THE FIELDS OF LITERATURE OR ECONOMICS, MEDICINE or peace, physics or chemistry, the winners of the Nobel Prize are fêted internationally for their expertise. But once the awards announcement has been made, the party is only just starting in Sweden…

The festivities were first broadcast on Swedish television in 1950, after years of radio-only transmissions. Gradually, people began dressing up in their own

Nobel banquet, 1958.

homes to celebrate in tandem with the 1,300 of the great and the good of Swedish society enjoying their luxurious meal in the Blue Hall at Stockholm's City Hall. Alternative banquets are now also held in schools and in a range of other societies from the Scouts to the Swedish Temperance Organisation, with attendees either in traditional folk costumes or in straightforward smart apparel. Schoolchildren often dress up, too – young girls in ball gowns, young boys in jacket and tie. Imagine a Eurovision Song Contest party in your home, but without the music.

The banquet itself has been held since 1901, when it was an all-male affair for 113 diners. In the early years, guests were seated at horseshoe-shaped tables, but as the numbers have grown so long tables have come in, surrounding a table of honour in the middle. One ongoing tradition is the flower decoration. Some 23,000 orchids, roses and gladioli are brought in from Sanremo, Italy, where Alfred Nobel lived towards the end of his life.

Although couples are not generally seated together (that includes the King and Queen), there are very few rules. The menu is a secret until it is revealed at 7 p.m. on 10 December, the day of the feast. And for many years, ice cream was always the pudding, with waiters, waitresses and folk musicians putting on a special 'ice cream parade' down the hall's impressive staircase.

Over the years the number of courses has dropped from five in 1901 (when the menu included brill and grouse breast) down to four after 1919 and three after 1945. The 1946 dinner was the first to start a lasting custom of bringing in elements of Scandinavian gastronomy, including roasted fillet of reindeer with lingonberry sauce.

Generally, the menu is fairly luxurious. Here, for example, is 2017's offering:

Pressed and dried Jerusalem artichoke, served with kohlrabi flowers,
flavoured with ginger and lightly roasted cabbage broth

Crispy saddle of lamb, potato terrine with Svedjan crème, yellow beet,
salt-baked celeriac, apple salad and rosemary-spiced lamb gravy

Frosty bilberry bavaroise, bilberry ice cream with lemon thyme,
lime jelly, lime curd and lime meringues

Taittinger Brut Réserve
Domini la Cartoixa Formiga de Vellut 2014
Viña Errázuriz Late Harvest Sauvignon Blanc 2016

Grönstedts Extra Cognac
Facile Punsch
Stenkulla Brunn Mineral Water

Shopping for 1,300 is a considerable exercise. The Nobel Foundation gives an example of a typical shopping list: 2,692 pigeon breasts, 475 lobster tails, 100kg of potatoes, 70 litres of sweet-and-sour raspberry-vinegar sauce, 67kg of Jerusalem artichokes, 53kg of Philadelphia cheese, 45kg of lightly smoked salmon.
Looking back over more than a century of menus, several trends are clear to see. The popular consommé and turtle soup starters are now things of the past. Béarnaise sauce has fallen out of fashion, Nordic berries are on the up. The Foundation is also keen to keep in step with the times. There were no banquets during either world war, the money instead donated to the Red Cross. And in 1947 they were keen not to be over-indulgent, hence the inclusion of sandwiches as a starter in the menu on the previous page. The single main course was chicken in a cream sauce, a dish that tips its hat to the simple, traditional farm diet, featuring potatoes, onions, carrots and cream. ◈

APPLE AND PRUNE PASTE

MAKES 12–16 SQUARES

1kg (35¼ oz) cooking apples
500g (17½oz) soft Agen prunes, stones removed
1 teaspoon cinnamon
¼ teaspoon clove
½ teaspoon allspice
800g (28oz) preserving sugar
drizzle of oil for greasing

Chop the apples, but don't bother to peel or remove the core as this helps with the setting process. Add the dried prunes along with the spices and cover the fruit halfway with water (about 1 pint or 600 ml). Cook on a low simmer, partially covered for 30–40 minutes until the fruit is very soft and turned to a pulp.

Set a sieve over a bowl and pass the fruits through, pushing with the back of a metal spoon.

Weigh the purée. Use 80g (2¾oz) of sugar to every 150g (5½oz) of puree you have. Transfer the purée and sugar to a heavy-based pan. Turn the heat to very low and allow the sugar to dissolve in the puree while stirring. Simmer very gently for 1 hour, stirring very regularly as this does catch and burn easily. The paste is ready when you can draw a wooden spoon through the mix, and it leaves a clear line on the bottom of the pan.

Grease a 20cm (8in) square cake tin with a little flavourless oil and line with parchment paper.

Spoon the paste into the prepared tin and tap it hard onto the surface so it is nice and even. Allow to cool before putting into the fridge to set overnight (or 12 hours).

Portion the paste once set and dust with caster sugar.

Wrap the squares in parchment paper and store in an airtight container for up to 3 months. Serve on a cheese board with liver pâté on toast or as an accompaniment to game.

MITTERRAND'S LAST – ILLEGAL – DINNER

1995

THE MOST FAMOUS FINAL MEAL OF THE TWENTIETH CENTURY WAS CONSUMED on New Year's Eve, 1995.

French President François Mitterrand was diagnosed with cancer in the early 1980s but managed to keep it a secret from the public for a decade while he remained in power. But once the great statesman realised he was near to death, he decided to invite 30 of his closest friends to a last supper…

Most of the menu he selected was straightforward (although the number of oysters he stuffed in – and the speed at which he did so – alarmed those present). Lightly fried foie gras had been one of his favourite dishes as president. Capon is a popular feast dish. The controversial choice was the final element, the ortolans.

These are tiny, yellow-throated songbirds (*Emberiza hortulana*), seen as representatives of the French spirit. Hunting them is banned by the EU and a major official crackdown on poachers began in France in summer 2017, although in practice a blind eye has often been turned to the birds' capture. Certainly ortolans are still commonly eaten, often at the end of a large family lunch towards the end of summer. As a measure of their popularity, there has been an estimated 80 per cent decline in their numbers since 1980. Ambelopoulia is a similar, Cypriot, dish of songbirds, and is equally illegal.

Readers who are fond of songbirds may want to turn the page now to avoid details of how ortolans are usually prepared.

The birds are caught in nets called matoles, mainly in the Landes region in the south-west of the country, as they migrate to Africa. In Provence, hunters also put glue on the branches of trees to capture them (as do The Twits in Roald Dahl's children's story of the same name). The ortolans are then kept in darkened cages and force-fed millet to fatten them up, sometimes until they double in size. Legend has it that ancient Roman emperors had the birds blinded to encourage

Preparation and tasting of ortolans by the Brotherhood Of the Ortolan, Tartas, France.

them to eat constantly throughout the day.

The bird is killed, traditionally by drowning in Armagnac, which also serves as a marinade. It is then plucked, placed in a cassoulet dish with a little salt and pepper, and roasted for around eight minutes. It is brought to the table in the dish, very hot and crispy.

Each diner then drapes an embroidered white napkin over their head, creating an intimate tent space that is supposed to accentuate the smell and taste of the experience, but also, some say, to stop God seeing what

MENU

Marennes oysters

Foie gras

Capon

Ortolans

Sauternes and red wine

they're about to do. As a bonus, it covers up what is quite a messy business.

The diner picks up the bird and bites its head off. Some people eat the head, but most leave it with the beak on the side of the plate. Then the whole thing is popped into the mouth feet first – wings, bones, innards, everything – and munched to a paste. Some people spit out the bigger bones. It takes about ten minutes to devour one properly.

Mitterrand was not the only ortolan-eater on that New Year's Eve. A platter of them had been prepared, not quite enough for each invitee, but still plenty. Mitterrand had two.

In the days after this New Year's Eve feast, he had a little tea and soup, but nothing more.

A week later he was dead. ◈

MOTO'S EDIBLE MENU

2005

TASTING MENUS ARE ONE THING, TASTY ONES ARE QUITE ANOTHER. IN THE increasingly high-tech world of gastronomy (see Last Dinner at elBulli, page 57), one of the giants was Homaru Cantu (1976–2015), who not only looked into levitating food and cooking with lasers, but also came up with the novel idea of a menu card you could actually eat.

Cantu worked with NASA to build a modified Canon inkjet printer (which he called the 'food replicator', as a tribute to Star Trek). Then, on a sheet of paper made of soybean and corn/potato starch, he printed the list of dishes to be served using an ink made from carrots, tomatoes, purple potatoes and other fruits and vegetables. This was then stuck onto a large tortilla chip and presented to diners at his restaurant, Moto, in Chicago.

Diners could simply munch on the menu or tear it into little pieces to add to a risotto or gazpacho, transforming it into 'alphabet soup'. Menus printed on croutons could also be added. The menus were sometimes flavoured to match a specific dish, so that one infused with dehydrated squash and sour cream would go with an appropriate soup.

Cantu took the concept a stage further with edible photos, one of a cow that tasted like steak, another of maki rolls that tasted of sesame, seaweed and soy sauce. He also envisioned magazine advertisements for pizza that could be ripped out and eaten as a taster.

Menus were not always on paper and could be 'written' on other items, such as a plate of crème fraîche. ◈

WORLD'S FIRST DOG-RESTAURANT MENU

Lily's Kitchen Diner, London, 2010

Once upon a time, the best a dog could hope for when it took its humans to an inn for lunch after a long walk was a bowl of water and the occasional furtive titbit, maybe a bone if the landlord was generous.

But over the last decade, dogs' dinners have improved dramatically to the point where they can now eat in their own dedicated restaurants. The first of these was the pop-up Lily's Kitchen Diner, which opened in 2010 on Pimlico Road in London, largely to advertise its new range of organic dog (and cat) food. Opening day was a big success with 30 dogs – six at a time, including a chihuahaua and a Great Dane – sitting down to enjoy their marigold petals and celery seeds out of thick white paper bowls set in holes at the tables.

Since then there have been several more openings, including another in London, The Curious Canine Kitchen in Bethnal Green (featuring tripe with seaweed and kale puree, gluten-free cinnamon quinoa biscuits and artisan marrowbones), and Boris & Horton in New York, where cats are banned and dogs must be on leashes if they want to indulge in delights such as bacon-topped cupcakes.

There has also been a sharp rise in the number of pubs and restaurants offering food for dogs alongside the

Lily's Kitchen Diner, London.

Lily's Kitchen Menu

For Dogs

SLOW-COOKED LAMB HOTPOT
BEEF & VEGETABLE DINNER
HOMESTYLE CHICKEN & TURKEY CASSEROLE
GOOSE & DUCK FEAST WITH FRUITS
CHICKEN & SPELT SUPPER
LAMB & SPELT SUPPER
ORGANIC DINNER FOR PUPPIES
CHICKEN & VEGETABLE BAKE
CHEESE & APPLE TREATS
BEEF & SPELT SUPPER
BEDTIME BISCUITS
FREE-RANGE RAWHIDE CHEWS

For Cats

ORGANIC DINNER with FISH for CATS
ORGANIC DINNER with CHICKEN for CATS
ORGANIC DINNER with LAMB for CATS
ORGANIC DINNER for KITTENS

more conventional human offering. Here's the Mutt's Menu from the King's Head in Woodbridge, Suffolk, introduced in 2011 (all items £1):

Cow ears
Pig ears
Honey-dried pig snout
Knotted bone
Doggy sausage
Ramekin of pedigree gravy bones

And around the UK, dogs can also now settle down to everything from 'hot dog without the bun cut up' (the Winged Ox, Glasgow, which also offers free beer to all dogs over 25) and liver brownies (the Dirty Onion, Belfast) to pupcakes (Pups and Cups Bistro, Liverpool). ◈

IKEA

Menu of the Future

ALTHOUGH THERE ARE INTERNATIONAL VARIATIONS, SHOPPERS AT IKEA around the world are most likely to enjoy a menu of Swedish meatballs with mashed potatoes, gravy and lingonberry jam, followed perhaps by some Daim cake (and an extraordinarily cheap sneaky hot dog on the way out). But IKEA is taking a long view about its offering.

IKEA Food have been coming up with such treats as vegan meatballs made from root vegetables – Grönsaksbullar – in 2015. However, their new fast-food menu of the future goes several insect-shaped steps further as part of their worthy aim to 'come up with dishes that look good, taste good and are good for people and planet', and the food scientists at SPACE10 – the company's Copenhagen-based innovation research and design laboratory – have been hard at work in its test kitchens. Salad is, of course, also on the potential menu, grown

IKEA Neatballs.

hydroponically in water rather than soil. Nothing worrying there.

And who's up for a Dogless Hotdog? This is made of dried and glazed baby carrots, beet and berry ketchup, mustard and turmeric cream, roasted onions, cucumber salad and a herb salad mix. It comes in a bun made of spirulina micro-algae which was once popular among the Aztecs and is on the list for possible menus for any Mars missions.

Arguably more controversial is the Bug Burger. Most people will be fine about the beetroot, parsnip and potato ingredients, but maybe a deal-breaker for some diners (though not those from Southeast Asia, where they are popular) are the 50g of mealworms in each portion. Mealworms are also a major ingredient of the Neatball.

To finish it all off, the Jetsons-style shoppers could also enjoy some microgreen ice cream made, again by hydroponics, from fennel, coriander, basil and mint.

Sadly, there are no immediate plans to add these to IKEA's menu. But we live in hope. ◈

INDEX

Academy Awards 105–6, 114
Adrià, Ferran 57–9
Alcatraz Prison 96–8
Aldrin, Buzz 27
Ali, Muhammad 107–9
Amundsen, Roald 17
Armstrong, Neil 27, 30
Astérix 174–7
Auschwitz-Birkenau 134–5
Aztecs 184, 221

Babette's Feast 114–17
Bastianich, Lidia 190
Beeton, Mrs Isabella 163–5
Berogno, Marta 180
Blowitz, Henri Opper de 9, 11
Blue Pheasant Tea Room 48–9
Brewer, Lawrence Russell 202–3
Bubwith, Nicholas 89–91
Bundy, Ted 202
Burns, Robert 92–3
Burns Night 92–3
Butlin, Billy 107, 109
Byron, Lord 76

Café Royal 136–9
Cantu, Homaru 217
Carlo Alberto, King 69–71
Cerf, Bennett Alfred 172–3
Cesare Borgia 191
Charles, Prince 102–3
Choron, Alexandre Étienne 208
Christmas 7, 94–8, 16
Clement VI, Pope 190–1
Coleridge-Taylor, Samuel 162
Communist Party of Great Britain 76–7
Concorde 28–9
Croly, Jane Cunningham 43

David Kalakaua, King of Hawaii 80
Delmonico's 43, 166–8
Diana, Princess 102–3
Dickens, Charles 7, 43, 94–5, 166–8, 193
Dr Seuss 172–3
dogs 218–19
Dudley, Robert 64–5

Egyptians, ancient 149–51
elBulli 57–9
Elizabeth, Queen Mother 80–1
Elizabeth I 64–5
Elizabeth II 84, 102, 111, 136, 190
Eltham Ordinances 61–3
Erhard, Ludwig 81
Everest, Mount 24–5

Facebook 120
1st Australian Imperial Force (AIF) 132–3
fish and chips 38–41
Florida State Prison 202–3
Francis, Pope 190–1

Gagarin, Yuri 27, 30
George IV 36, 66–8, 123
George VI 80–1, 102, 103
Goebbels, Joseph 23
Golden Temple, India 181–3
Google 120
Grahame, Kenneth 169–71
Green Eggs and Ham 172–3
Gurney, Ivor 128, 129, 131

Hampstead Communist Party 76–7
Harry, Prince 103
Haus Hiltl 44–7
Helgesen, Henry T. 14
Henry IV 61, 89
Henry VIII 61–3
Hiawatha 161–2
Hill, Octavia 169–70
Hillary, Sir Edmund 24–5
Hiltl, Ambrosius 45
Hindenburg 21–3
Hormel Foods 112
Hotel Cecil 78–9
House of the Buffet Supper 158–9
Housekeepers' Club 48–9
Hugo, Victor 207, 208
Hunt, Colonel John 24, 25

IKEA 220–1
Independence Day (India) 82–3
Indian restaurants 35–7
International Space Station 27, 30–3

Jesus 179–80
Johnson, Lyndon 81

Khomeini, Ayatollah 87
Klyshko, Nikolai 76
Korean Peace Summit 140–3

Labouchère, Henry 208
Ladies' Luncheon 42–3
langar 181–3
Langston, Mary Jenkins 100
Lashly, William 16–17
the Last Supper 179–80, 188
Le Club des Chefs des Chefs 140
Leonardo da Vinci 179–80
Lily's Kitchen Diner 218–19
Lincoln, Abraham 185, 187
Longfellow, Henry Wadsworth 161
Lyons' Corner House 54–6, 74

McDonald's 50–3
MacFarlane, Flora 48
McGovern, Dr Patrick 152, 154
Mahomed, Sake Dean 35–6
Matterer, James 90
Mentuwoser 149–51
Midas, King 152–5
the Minerva 72, 74
Mitterrand, François 214–16
Monty Python 112–13
Moto 217
Mukund, Anupama 158–9

Nagelmackers, Georges 9
Naidu, Sarojini 82
Nair, Billy 201
Native Americans 161–2
Neanderthals 145–6
Nobel Prize 210–13
Norgay, Tenzing 24–5
Olympics 118–19
Orient Express 9–13
ortolans 214–16
Otzi the Iceman 147–8

Pahlavi, Shah Mohammad Reza 84–7
Paris, siege of 207–9
Parker, 'Colonel Tom' 99
Paul, Hamilton 92–3
Peake, Tim 27
Peary, Robert Edwin 14–15
Pepys, Samuel 89, 205–6
Persian Empire 84–7
Pethick, Emmeline 79
Pethick-Lawrence, Frederick 78, 79
picnics 169–71
pineapple 66, 68
Pixar Studios 120–1
Presley, Elvis and Priscilla 99–101
Press Club 166–8
Puck, Wolfgang 106

Ranhofer, Charles 168
Rhondda, Viscountess 78–9
Robben Island 200–1
Romans 156–9
Romney's 25
Roosevelt, Franklin 80–1

Sahagún, Bernardino de 184
Salter, William 127
school dinners 196–9
Scott, Captain Robert Falcon 16–17, 24, 147
Sibbet, Robert 207
Smollett, Tobias 93
space 26–7
SPAM® 112–13

Taj Mahal Palace Hotel 82–3
Thanksgiving 185–7
Thirteen Club 188–9
Titanic, RMS 18–20, 129
Tlacatlaolli 184

Urciuoli, Generoso 180

Varriano, John 180
vegetarian restaurants 44–7
Victoria, Queen 92, 94
Vitellius, Emperor 156–7, 158

Wansink, Brian 158–9
Weislogel, Andrew 158–9
Wellington, Duke of 123–7
Weyrich, Dr Laura 145, 146
William, Prince 103
William IV 36, 66
Wilson, Harold 107, 108, 132
The Wind in the Willows 169–71
Winslow, Edward 186
Wolsey, Cardinal 61, 62
Women's Freedom League 72–5, 78–9
workhouses 193–5
World Cup 110–11
World War I 128–31

Young, John 27

Zeppelin Airline Company 21–3

ACKNOWLEDGEMENTS

Thanks to Acadamia Barilla, Lydia Rousseau (for transcribing the menu from the original hand-written document which is in the archives at Stratfield Saye House), Jane Branfield and the Trustees of Stratfield Saye House, John Rix, and Heidemarie Rix-Anacker.

PHOTOGRAPHY CREDITS

Academia Barilla Gastronomic Library; Parma; Italy 4bl, 70; **Alamy Stock Photo** AF archive/ Dargaud Films/Les Productions René Goscinny/Studios Idefix/Halas and Batchelor Cartoon Films 175; Aflo Co Ltd 143; Allan Cash Picture Library 197; Archive PL 210; Art Collection 2 68; Betzer-Panorama Film/ Danish Film Institute/Nordisk/Entertainment Pictures 116; Chronicle 9, 194b; Dinodia 82; Everett Collection 51; FLHC 85 184; GL Archive 194a; Granger Historical Archive 19, 95, 166; Helene Rogers/Art Directors & TRIP 25; Heritage Image Partnership 156; History Collection 2016 7ar, 73, 79l & r; Interfoto 23; Military Images 130al; Shawshots 18, 20r; The Picture Art Collection 126; The Print Collector 17; Trinity Mirror/ Mirrorpix 107, 111; World History Archive 158, 186; **Bridgeman Images** Private Collection/The Stapleton Collection 171; Archives of **CIWL** © Wagons-Lits Diffusion; Paris 2017 10; **Dreamstime.com** Mehmet Doruk Taşcı 153; Tea 52; **Flickr** Lou Stejskal (CC BY 2.0) 217; **FotoLibra** Malcolm Warrington 55; 56; **Getty Images** Andrea Solero/AFP 148; Bettmann 99, 106; Bill Brandt 54; Culture Club 7al, 163; De Agostini 159; General Photographic Agency 40; Georges Galmiche/INA via Getty Images 4c; Harry Todd/Fox Photos 199; Hulton Archive 74; Jack Garofalo/Paris Match 86; Jacques Lange/Paris Match 215; Jewel Samad/AFP 191; Kyodo News 119; Maurice-Louis Branger/Roger Viollet 130ar; Peter Macdiarmid 218, 219; Photoquest 81; Popperfoto 38, 130b; Steve Larson/The Denver Post 172; The Print Collector 92; **Hiltl** 4ar & bc, 7bl, 44; 46; 47; **iStock** mazzzur 189; taffpix 26; **Library of Congress** 15; **Metropolitan Museum of Art** Gift of Edward S Harkness, 1912 4br, 150; **NASA** 30; **The National Archives** (E36-231 (40)) 63; **National Library of Australia** 4cl & cr, 133; © **National Maritime Museum**, Greenwich; London 201; **New York Public Library** Buttolph Collection 42, Digital Collections 189; **Python (Monty) Pictures Ltd** 113; **Royal Pavilion and Museums**; Brighton & Hove (CC BY SA) 36a; **Shutterstock** Betzer-Panorama Film/ Danish Film Institute/Kobal 115; Kharbine-Tapabor 12; **SPACE10** Kasper Kristoffersen 22 © **Stratfield Saye Preservation Trust** 127; **TopFoto** Roger Viollet 209; **Wikimedia Commons** 168; Alberto Fernandez Fernandez (CC BY-SA 3.0) 179; D Gordon E Robertson (CC BY-SA 3.0) 200; Simon Harriyott from Uckfield; England (CC BY 2.0) 7br, 36b; Stockholmskällan.se/Photo Brendler & Åkerberg 4al; Walker Art Gallery/Google Art Project 62.